KT-493-260

LIFE TOGETHER

DIETRICH BONHOEFFER

Life Together

SCM PRESS LTD

BLOOMSBURY STREET LONDON

First published under the title of
GEMEINSAMES LEBEN
by Chr. Kaiser Verlag, Munich

Translated
from the fifth edition (1949) by
John W. Doberstein

SBN 334 00904 9

First British edition 1954
Second impression 1956
Third impression 1960
Fourth impression 1962
Fifth impression 1963
Sixth impression 1965 (reset)
Seventh impression 1968
Eighth impression 1970
Ninth impression 1972

Printed in Great Britain by
Billing and Sons Limited
Guildford and London

CONTENTS

CONTENTS

I

COMMUNITY

I

Community

'BEHOLD, HOW good and how pleasant it is for brethren to dwell together in unity!' (Ps. 133.1). In the following we shall consider a number of directions and precepts that the Scriptures provide us for our life together under the Word.

It is not simply to be taken for granted that the Christian has the privilege of living among other Christians. Jesus Christ lived in the midst of his enemies. At the end all his disciples deserted him. On the Cross he was utterly alone, surrounded by evildoers and mockers. For this cause he had come, to bring peace to the enemies of God. So the Christian, too, belongs not in the seclusion of a cloistered life but in the thick of foes. There is his commission, his work. 'The Kingdom is to be in the midst of your enemies. And he who will not suffer this does not want to be of the Kingdom of Christ; he wants to be among friends, to sit among roses and lilies, not with the bad people but the devout people. O you blasphemers and betrayers of Christ! If Christ had done what you are doing who would ever have been spared?' (Luther).

'I will sow them among the people: and they shall remember me in far countries' (Zech. 10.9). According to God's will Christendom is a scattered people, scattered like seed 'into all the kingdoms of the earth' (Deut. 28.25). That is its curse and its promise. God's people must dwell in far countries among the unbelievers, but it will be the seed of the Kingdom of God in all the world.

'I will . . . gather them; for I have redeemed them:

. . . and they shall return' (Zech. 10.8, 9). When will that happen? It has happened in Jesus Christ, who died 'that he should gather together in one the children of God that were scattered abroad' (John 11.52), and it will finally occur visibly at the end of time when the angels of God 'shall gather together his elect from the four winds, from one end of heaven to the other' (Matt. 24.31). Until then, God's people remain scattered, held together solely in Jesus Christ, having become one in the fact that, dispersed among unbelievers, they remember *him* in the far countries.

So between the death of Christ and the Last Day it is only by a gracious anticipation of the last things that Christians are privileged to live in visible fellowship with other Christians. It is by the grace of God that a congregation is permitted to gather visibly in this world to share God's Word and sacrament. Not all Christians receive this blessing. The imprisoned, the sick, the scattered lonely, the proclaimers of the Gospel in heathen lands stand alone. They know that visible fellowship is a blessing. They remember, as the Psalmist did, how they went 'with the multitude . . . to the house of God, with the voice of joy and praise, with a multitude that kept holyday' (Ps. 42.4). But they remain alone in far countries, a scattered seed according to God's will. Yet what is denied them as an actual experience they seize upon more fervently in faith. Thus the exiled disciple of the Lord, John the Apocalyptist, celebrates in the loneliness of Patmos the heavenly worship with his congregations 'in the Spirit on the Lord's day' (Rev. 1.10). He sees the seven candlesticks, his congregations, the seven stars, the angels of the congregations, and in the midst and above it all the Son of Man, Jesus Christ, in all the splendour of the resurrection. He strengthens and fortifies him by his Word. This is the heavenly fellowship, shared by the exile on the day of his Lord's resurrection.

The physical presence of other Christians is a source of incomparable joy and strength to the believer. Longingly the imprisoned apostle Paul calls 'his dearly beloved son in the faith', Timothy to come to him in prison in the last days of his life; he would see him again and have him near. Paul has not forgotten the tears Timothy shed when last they parted (II Tim. 1.4). Remembering the congregation in Thessalonica, Paul prays 'night and day . . . exceedingly that we might see your face' (I Thess. 3.10). The aged John knows that his joy will not be full until he can come to his own people and speak face to face instead of writing with ink (II John 12).

The believer feels no shame, as though he were still living too much in the flesh, when he yearns for the physical presence of other Christians. Man was created a body, the Son of God appeared on earth in the body, he was raised in the body, in the sacrament the believer receives the Lord Christ in the body, and the resurrection of the dead will bring about the perfected fellowship of God's spiritual-physical creatures. The believer therefore lauds the Creator, the Redeemer, God, Father, Son and Holy Spirit, for the bodily presence of a brother. The prisoner, the sick person, the Christian in exile sees in the companionship of a fellow Christian a physical sign of the gracious presence of the triune God. Visitor and visited in loneliness recognize in each other the Christ who is present in the body; they receive and meet each other as one meets the Lord, in reverence, humility, and joy. They receive each other's benedictions as the benediction of the Lord Jesus Christ. But if there is so much blessing and joy even in a single encounter of brother with brother, how inexhaustible are the riches that open up for those who by God's will are privileged to live in the daily fellowship of life with other Christians!

It is true, of course, that what is an unspeakable gift of God for the lonely individual is easily disregarded and trodden under foot by those who have the gift every day. It is easily forgotten that the fellowship of Christian brethren is a gift of grace, a gift of the Kingdom of God that any day may be taken from us, that the time that still separates us from utter loneliness may be brief indeed. Therefore, let him who until now has had the privilege of living a common Christian life with other Christians praise God's grace from the bottom of his heart. Let him thank God on his knees and declare: It is grace, nothing but grace, that we are allowed to live in community with Christian brethren.

The measure with which God bestows the gift of visible community is varied. The Christian in exile is comforted by a brief visit of a Christian brother, a prayer together and a brother's blessing; indeed, he is strengthened by a letter written by the hand of a Christian. The greetings in the letters written with Paul's own hand were doubtless tokens of such community. Others are given the gift of common worship on Sundays. Still others have the privilege of living a Christian life in the fellowship of their families. Seminarians before their ordination receive the gift of common life with their brethren for a definite period. Among earnest Christians in the Church today there is a growing desire to meet together with other Christians in the rest periods of their work for common life under the Word. Communal life is again being recognized by Christians today as the grace that it is, as the extraordinary, the 'roses and lilies' of the Christian life.

Through and in Jesus Christ

Christianity means community through Jesus Christ and in Jesus Christ. No Christian community is more or less than this. Whether it be a brief, single encounter or the daily fellowship of years, Christian community is only this. We belong to one another only through and in Jesus Christ.

What does this mean? It means, first, that a Christian needs others because of Jesus Christ. It means, second, that a Christian comes to others only through Jesus Christ. It means, third, that in Jesus Christ we have been chosen from eternity, accepted in time, and united for eternity.

First, the Christian is the man who no longer seeks his salvation, his deliverance, his justification in himself, but in Jesus Christ alone. He knows that God's Word in Jesus Christ pronounces him guilty, even when he does not feel his guilt, and God's Word in Jesus Christ pronounces him not guilty and righteous, even when he does not feel that he is righteous at all. The Christian no longer lives of himself, by his own claims and his own justification, but by God's claims and God's justification. He lives wholly by God's Word pronounced upon him, whether that Word declares him guilty or innocent.

The death and the life of the Christian is not determined by his own resources; rather he finds both only in the Word that comes to him from the outside, in God's Word to him. The Reformers expressed it this way: Our righteousness is an 'alien righteousness' a righteousness that comes from outside of us (*extra nos*). They were saying that the Christian is dependent on the Word of God spoken to him. He is pointed outward, to the Word that comes to him. The Christian lives wholly by the truth of God's Word in Jesus Christ. If somebody asks him, Where is your salvation, your righteousness? he can never point to himself. He points to the Word of God in Jesus Christ, which assures him salvation and righteousness. He is as alert as possible to this Word. Because he daily hungers and thirsts for righteousness, he daily desires the redeeming Word. And it can come only from the outside. In himself he is destitute and dead. Help must come from the outside, and it has come and comes daily and anew in the Word of Jesus Christ, bringing redemption, righteousness, innocence, and blessedness.

But God has put this Word into the mouth of men in order that it may be communicated to other men. When one person is struck by the Word, he speaks it to others. God has willed that we should seek him and find his living

Word in the witness of a brother, in the mouth of a man. Therefore, a Christian needs another Christian who speaks God's Word to him. He needs him again and again when he becomes uncertain and discouraged, for by himself he cannot help himself without belying the truth. He needs his brother man as a bearer and proclaimer of the divine word of salvation. He needs his brother solely because of Jesus Christ. The Christ in his own heart is weaker than the Christ in the word of his brother; his own heart is uncertain, his brother's is sure.

And that also clarifies the goal of all Christian community: they meet one another as bringers of the message of salvation. As such, God permits them to meet together and gives them community. Their fellowship is founded solely upon Jesus Christ and this 'alien righteousness'. All we can say, therefore, is: the community of Christians springs solely from the biblical and Reformation message of the justification of man through grace alone; this alone is the basis of the longing of Christians for one another.

Second, a Christian comes to others only through Jesus Christ. Among men there is strife. 'He is our peace', says Paul of Jesus Christ (Eph. 2.14). Without Christ there is discord between God and man and between man and man. Christ became the Mediator and made peace with God and among men. Without Christ we should not know God and could not call upon him, nor come to him. But without Christ we would also not know our brother, nor could we come to him. The way is blocked by our own ego. Christ opened up the way to God and to our brother. Now Christians can live with one another in peace; they can love and serve one another; they can become one. But they can continue to do so only by way of Jesus Christ. Only in Jesus Christ are we one, only through him are we bound together. To eternity he remains the one Mediator.

Third, when God's Son took on flesh, he truly and bodily took on, out of pure grace, our being, our nature, ourselves. This was the eternal counsel of the triune God. Now we are in him. Where he is, there we are too, in the incarnation, on the Cross, and in his resurrection. We belong to him because we are in him. That is why the Scriptures call us the Body of Christ. But if, before we could know and wish it, we have been chosen and accepted with the whole Church in Jesus Christ, then we also belong to him in eternity *with* one another. We who live here in fellowship with him will one day be with him in eternal fellowship. He who looks upon his brother should know that he will be eternally united with him in Jesus Christ. Christian community means community through and in Jesus Christ. On this presupposition rests everything that the Scriptures provide in the way of directions and precepts for the communal life of Christians.

'But as touching brotherly love ye need not that I write unto you: for ye yourselves are taught of God to love one another . . . but we beseech you, brethren, that ye increase more and more' (I Thess. 4.9, 10). God himself has undertaken to teach brotherly love; all that men can add to it is to remember this divine instruction and the admonition to excel in it more and more. When God was merciful, when he revealed Jesus Christ to us as our Brother, when he won our hearts by his love, this was the beginning of our instruction in divine love. When God was merciful to us, we learned to be merciful with our brethren. When we received forgiveness instead of judgment, we, too, were made ready to forgive our brethren. What God did to us, we then owed to others. The more we received, the more we were able to give; and the more meagre our brotherly love, the less were we living by God's mercy and love. Thus God himself taught us to meet one another as God has met us in Christ. 'Wherefore receive ye one another, as Christ also received us to the glory of God' (Rom. 15.7).

In this wise does one, whom God has placed in common life with other Christians, learn what it means to have brothers. 'Brethren in the Lord', Paul calls his congregation (Phil. 1.14). One is a brother to another only through Jesus

Christ. I am a brother to another person through what Jesus Christ did for me and to me; the other person has become a brother to me through what Jesus Christ did for him. This fact that we are brethren only through Jesus Christ is of immeasurable significance. Not only the other person who is earnest and devout, who comes to me seeking brotherhood, must I deal with in fellowship. My brother is rather that other person who has been redeemed by Christ, delivered from sin, and called to faith and eternal life. Not what a man is in himself as a Christian, his spirituality and piety, constitutes the basis of our community. What determines our brotherhood is what that man is by reason of Christ. Our community with one another consists solely in what Christ has done to both of us. This is true not merely at the beginning, as though in the course of time something else were to be added to our community; it remains so for all the future and to all eternity. I have community with others and I shall continue to have it only through Jesus Christ. The more genuine and the deeper our community becomes, the more will everything else between us recede, the more clearly and purely will Jesus Christ and his work become the one and only thing that is vital between us. We have one another only through Christ, but through Christ we do have one another, wholly, and for all eternity.

That dismisses once and for all every clamorous desire for something more. One who wants more than what Christ has established does not want Christian brotherhood. He is looking for some extraordinary social experience which he has not found elsewhere; he is bringing muddled and impure desires into Christian brotherhood. Just at this point Christian brotherhood is threatened most often at the very start by the greatest danger of all, the danger of being poisoned at its root, the danger of confusing Christian brotherhood with some wishful idea of religious fellowship, of confounding the natural desire of the devout heart for community with the spiritual reality of Christian brotherhood. In Christian brotherhood everything depends upon its being clear right from the beginning, *first, that Christian brotherhood is not an ideal, but a divine reality. Second, that Christian brotherhood is a spiritual and not a psychic reality.*

Not an Ideal but a Divine Reality

Innumerable times a whole Christian community has broken down because it had sprung from a wish dream. The serious Christian, set down for the first time in a Christian community, is likely to bring with him a very definite idea of what Christian life together should be and try to realize it. But God's grace speedily shatters such dreams. Just as surely God desires to lead us to a knowledge of genuine Christian fellowship, so surely must we be overwhelmed by a great general disillusionment with others, with Christians in general, and, if we are fortunate, with ourselves.

By sheer grace God will not permit us to live even for a brief period in a dream world. He does not abandon us to those rapturous experiences and lofty moods that come over us like a dream. God is not a God of the emotions but the God of truth. Only that fellowship which faces sucn disillusionment, with all its unhappy and ugly aspects, begins to be what it should be in God's sight, begins to grasp in faith the promise that is given to it. The sooner this shock of disillusionment comes to an individual and to a community the better for both. A community which cannot bear and cannot survive such a crisis, which insists upon keeping its illusion when it should be shattered, permanently loses in that moment the promise of Christian community. Sooner or later it will collapse. Every human wish dream that is injected into the Christian community is a hindrance to genuine community and must be banished if genuine community is to survive. He who loves his dream of a community more than the Christian community itself becomes a destroyer of the latter, even though his personal

intentions may be ever so honest and earnest and sacri-
ficial.

God hates visionary dreaming; it makes the dreamer
proud and pretentious. The man who fashions a visionary
ideal of community demands that it be realized by God, by
others, and by himself. He enters the community of Christians with his demands, sets up his own law, and judges the
brethren and God himself accordingly. He stands adamant,
a living reproach to all others in the circle of brethren. He
acts as if he is the creator of the Christian community, as if
his dream binds men together. When things do not go his
way, he calls the effort a failure. When his ideal picture is
destroyed, he sees the community going to smash. So he
becomes, first an accuser of his brethren, then an accuser
of God, and finally the despairing accuser of himself.

Because God has already laid the only foundation of our
fellowship, because God has bound us together in one body
with other Christians in Jesus Christ, long before we
entered into common life with them, we enter into that
common life not as demanders but as thankful recipients.
We thank God for what he has done for us. We thank God
for giving us brethren who live by his call, by his forgiveness, and his promise. We do not complain of what God
does not give us; we rather thank God for what he does
give us daily. And is not what has been given us enough :
brothers, who will go on living with us through sin and
need under the blessing of his grace? Is the divine gift of
Christian fellowship anything less than this, any day, even
the most difficult and distressing day? Even when sin and
misunderstanding burden the communal life, is not the
sinning brother still a brother, with whom I, too, stand
under the Word of Christ? Will not his sin be a constant
occasion for me to give thanks that both of us may live in
the forgiving love of God in Jesus Christ? Thus the very
hour of disillusionment with my brother becomes incom-
parably salutary, because it so thoroughly teaches me that
neither of us can ever live by our own words and deeds, but

only by that one Word and Deed which really binds us together—the forgiveness of sins in Jesus Christ. When the morning mists of dreams vanish, then dawns the bright day of Christian fellowship.

In the Christian community thankfulness is just what it is anywhere else in the Christian life. Only he who gives thanks for little things receives the big things. We prevent God from giving us the great spiritual gifts he has in store for us, because we do not give thanks for daily gifts. We think we dare not be satisfied with the small measure of spiritual knowledge, experience, and love that has been given to us, and that we must constantly be looking forward eagerly for the highest good. Then we deplore the fact that we lack the deep certainty, the strong faith, and the rich experience that God has given to others, and we consider this lament to be pious. We pray for the big things and forget to give thanks for the ordinary, small (and yet really not small) gifts. How can God entrust great things to one who will not thankfully receive from him the little things? If we do not give thanks daily for the Christian fellowship in which we have been placed, even where there is no great experience, no discoverable riches, but much weakness, small faith, and difficulty; if, on the contrary, we only keep complaining to God that everything is so paltry and petty, so far from what we expected, then we hinder God from letting our fellowship grow according to the measure and riches which are there for us all in Jesus Christ.

This applies in a special way to the complaints often heard from pastors and zealous members about their congregations. A pastor should not complain about his congregation, certainly never to other people, but also not to God. A congregation has not been entrusted to him in order that he should become its accuser before God and men. When a person becomes alienated from a Christian community in which he has been placed and begins to raise complaints about it, he had better examine himself first to see whether the trouble is not due to his wish dream that should be shattered by God; and if this be the case, let him thank God for leading him into this predicament. But if not, let him nevertheless guard against ever becoming an accuser of the congregation before God. Let him rather accuse himself for his unbelief. Let him pray God for an understanding of his own failure and his particular sin, and pray that he may not wrong his brethren. Let him, in the consciousness of his own guilt, make intercession for his brethren. Let him do what he is committed to do, and thank God.

Christian community is like the Christian's sanctification. It is a gift of God which we cannot claim. Only God knows the real state of our fellowship, of our sanctification. What may appear weak and trifling to us may appear great and glorious to God. Just as the Christian should not be constantly feeling his spiritual pulse, so, too, the Christian community has not been given to us by God for us to be constantly taking its temperature. The more thankfully we daily receive what is given to us, the more surely and steadily will fellowship increase and grow from day to day as God pleases.

Christian brotherhood is not an ideal which we must realize; it is rather a reality created by God in Christ in which we may participate. The more clearly we learn to recognize that the ground and strength and promise of all our fellowship is in Jesus Christ alone, the more serenely shall we think of our fellowship and pray and hope for it.

A Spiritual not a Human Reality

Because Christian community is founded solely on Jesus Christ, it is a spiritual and not a psychic reality. In this it differs absolutely from all other communities. The Scriptures call 'pneumatic', 'spiritual', that which is created only by the Holy Spirit, who puts Jesus Christ into our hearts as Lord and Saviour. The Scriptures term 'psychic', 'human',[1] that which comes from the natural urges, powers, and capacities of the human spirit.

The basis of all spiritual reality is the clear, manifest Word of God in Jesus Christ. The basis of all human reality is the dark turbid urges and desires of the human mind. The basis of the community of the Spirit is truth; the basis of human community of spirit is desire. The essence of the community of the Spirit is light, for 'God is light, and in him is no darkness at all' (I John 1.5) and 'if we walk in the light, as he is in the light, we have fellowship one with another' (1.7). The essence of human community of spirit is darkness, 'for from within, out of the heart of men, proceed evil thoughts' (Mark 7.21). It is the deep night that hovers over the sources of all human action, even over all noble and devout impulses. The community of the Spirit is the fellowship of those who are called by Christ; human community of spirit is the fellowship of devout souls. In the community of the Spirit there burns the bright love of brotherly service, *agape*; in human community of spirit there glows the dark love of good and evil desire, *eros*. In the former there is ordered, brotherly service, in the latter disordered desire for pleasure; in the former humble subjection to the brethren, in the latter humble yet haughty subjection of a brother to one's own desire. In the community of the Spirit the Word of God alone rules; in human community of spirit there rules, along with the Word, the man who is furnished with exceptional powers, experience, and magical suggestive capacities. There God's Word alone is binding; here, besides the Word, men bind others to themselves. There all power honour, and dominion are surrendered to the Holy Spirit; here spheres of power and influence of a personal nature are sought and cultivated. It is true, in so far as these are devout men, that

[1] For the sake of clarity, liberty has been taken in the following pages to render the term *'geistlich'* as 'spiritual', referring to the Holy Spirit, and the term *'seelisch'* as 'human', rather than employ the terms 'pneumatic' and 'psychic', which are precise but perhaps alien to our ears.—*Tr.*

they do this with the intention of serving the highest and the best, but in actuality the result is to dethrone the Holy Spirit, to relegate him to remote unreality. In actuality, it is only the human that is operative here. In the spiritual realm the Spirit governs; in human community, psychological techniques and methods. In the former naïve, un-psychological, unmethodical, helping love is extended towards one's brother; in the latter psychological analysis and construction; in the one the service of one's brother is simple and humble; in the other service consists of a searching, calculating analysis of a stranger.

Perhaps the contrast between spiritual and human reality can be made most clear in the following observation: Within the spiritual community there is never, nor in any way, any 'immediate' relationship of one to another, whereas human community expresses a profound, elemental, human desire for community, for immediate contact with other human souls, just as in the flesh there is the urge for physical merger with other flesh. Such desire of the human soul seeks a complete fusion of I and Thou, whether this occur in the union of love or, what is after all the same thing, in the forcing of another person into one's sphere of power and influence. Here is where the humanly strong person is in his element, securing for himself the admiration, the love, or the fear of the weak. Here human ties, suggestions, and bonds are everything, and in the immediate community of souls we have reflected the distorted image of everything that is originally and solely peculiar to community mediated through Christ.

Thus there is such a thing as human absorption. It appears in all the forms of conversion wherever the superior power of one person is consciously or unconsciously misused to influence profoundly and draw into his spell another individual or a whole community. Here one soul operates directly upon another soul. The weak have been overcome by the strong, the resistance of the weak has broken down under the influence of another person. He has been overpowered, but not won over by the thing itself. This becomes evident as soon as the demand is made that he throw himself into the cause itself, independently of the person to whom he is bound, or possibly in opposition to this person. Here is where the humanly converted person breaks down and thus makes it evident that his conversion was effected, not by the Holy Spirit, but by a man, and therefore has no stability.

Likewise, there is a human love of one's neighbour. Such passion is capable of prodigious sacrifices. Often it far surpasses genuine Christian love in fervent devotion and visible results. It speaks the Christian language with overwhelming and stirring eloquence. But it is what Paul is speaking of when he says: 'And though I bestow my goods to feed the poor, and though I give my body to be burned' —in other words, though I combine the utmost deeds of love with the utmost of devotion—'and have not charity [that is, the love of Christ], it profiteth me nothing' (I Cor. 13.3). Human love is directed to the other person for his own sake, spiritual love loves him for Christ's sake. Therefore, human love seeks direct contact with the other person; it loves him not as a free person but as one whom it binds to itself. It wants to gain, to capture by every means; it uses force. It desires to be irresistible, to rule.

Human love has little regard for truth. It makes the truth relative, since nothing, not even the truth, must come between it and the beloved person. Human love desires the other person, his company, his answering love, but it does not serve him. On the contrary, it continues to desire even when it seems to be serving. There are two marks, both of which are one and the same thing, that manifest the difference between spiritual and human love: Human love cannot tolerate the dissolution of a fellowship that has become false for the sake of genuine fellowship, and human love cannot love an enemy, that is, one who seriously and stubbornly resists it. Both spring from the same source: human love is by its very nature desire—

desire for human community. So long as it can satisfy this desire in some way, it will not give it up, even for the sake of truth, even for the sake of genuine love for others. But where it can no longer expect its desire to be fulfilled, there it stops short—namely, in the face of an enemy. There it turns into hatred, contempt, and calumny.

Right here is the point where spiritual love begins. This is why human love becomes personal hatred when it encounters genuine spiritual love, which does not desire but serves. Human love makes itself an end in itself. It creates of itself an end, an idol which it worships, to which it must subject everything. It nurses and cultivates an ideal, it loves itself, and nothing else in the world. Spiritual love, however, comes from Jesus Christ, it serves him alone; it knows that it has no immediate access to other persons.

Jesus Christ stands between the lover and the others he loves. I do not know in advance what love of others means on the basis of the general idea of love that grows out of my human desires—all this may rather be hatred and an insidious kind of selfishness in the eyes of Christ. What love is, only Christ tells in his Word. Contrary to all my own opinions and convictions, Jesus Christ will tell me what love toward the brethren really is. Therefore, spiritual love is bound solely to the Word of Jesus Christ. Where Christ bids me to maintain fellowship for the sake of love, I will maintain it. Where his truth enjoins me to dissolve a fellowship for love's sake, there I will dissolve it, despite all the protests of my human love. Because spiritual love does not desire but rather serves, it loves an enemy as a brother. It originates neither in the brother nor in the enemy but in Christ and his Word. Human love can never understand spiritual love, for spiritual love is from above; it is something completely strange, new, and incomprehensible to all earthly love.

Because Christ stands between me and others, I dare not desire direct fellowship with them. As only Christ can speak to me in such a way that I may be saved, so others, too, can be saved only by Christ himself. This means that I must release the other person from every attempt of mine to regulate, coerce, and dominate him with my love. The other person needs to retain his independence of me; to be loved for what he is, as one for whom Christ became man, died, and rose again, for whom Christ bought forgiveness of sins and eternal life. Because Christ has long since acted decisively for my brother, before I could begin to act, I must leave him his freedom to be Christ's; I must meet him only as the person that he already is in Christ's eyes. This is the meaning of the proposition that we can meet others only through the mediation of Christ. Human love constructs its own image of the other person, of what he is and what he should become. It takes the life of the other person into its own hands. Spiritual love recognizes the true image of the other person which he has received from Jesus Christ; the image that Jesus Christ himself embodied and would stamp upon all men.

Therefore, spiritual love proves itself in that everything it says and does commends Christ. It will not seek to move others by all too personal, direct influence, by impure interference in the life of another. It will not take pleasure in pious, human fervour and excitement. It will rather meet the other person with the clear Word of God and be ready to leave him alone with this Word for a long time, willing to release him again in order that Christ may deal with him. It will respect the line that has been drawn between him and us by Christ, and it will find full fellowship with him in the Christ who alone binds us together. Thus this spiritual love will speak to Christ about a brother more than to a brother about Christ. It knows that the most direct way to others is always through prayer to Christ and that love of others is wholly dependent upon the truth in Christ. It is out of this love that John the disciple speaks. 'I have no greater joy than to hear that my children walk in truth' (III John 4).

Human love lives by uncontrolled and uncontrollable

dark *desires*; spiritual love lives in the clear light of service ordered by the *truth*. Human love produces human subjection, dependence, constraint; spiritual love creates *freedom* of the brethren under the Word. Human love breeds hothouse flowers; spiritual love creates the *fruits* that grow healthily in accord with God's good will in the rain and storm and sunshine of God's outdoors. The existence of any Christian life together depends on whether it succeeds at the right time in bringing out the ability to distinguish between a human ideal and God's reality, between spiritual and human community.

The life or death of a Christian community is determined by whether it achieves sober wisdom on this point as soon as possible. In other words, life together under the Word will remain sound and healthy only where it does not form itself into a movement, an order, a society, a *collegium pietatis*, but rather where it understands itself as being a part of the one, holy, catholic, Christian Church, where it shares actively and passively in the sufferings and struggles and promise of the whole Church. Every principle of selection and every separation connected with it that is not necessitated quite objectively by common work, local conditions, or family connections is of the greatest danger to a Christian community. When the way of intellectual or spiritual selection is taken the human element always insinuates itself and robs the fellowship of its spiritual power and effectiveness for the Church, drives it into sectarianism. The exclusion of the weak and insignificant, the seemingly useless people, from a Christian community may actually mean the exclusion of Christ; in the poor brother Christ is knocking at the door. We must, therefore, be very careful at this point.

The undiscerning observer may think that this mixture of ideal and reality, of the human and spiritual, is most likely to be present where there are a number of levels in the structure of a community, as in marriage, the family, friendship, where the human element as such already assumes a central importance in the community's coming into being at all, and where the spiritual is only something added to the physical and intellectual. According to this view, it is only in these relationships that there is a danger of confusing and mixing the two spheres, whereas there can be no such danger in a purely spiritual fellowship. This idea, however, is a great delusion. According to all experience the truth is just the opposite. A marriage, a family, a friendship is quite conscious of the limitations of its community-building power; such relationships know very well, if they are sound, where the human element stops and the spiritual begins. They know the difference between physical-intellectual and spiritual community. On the contrary, when a community of a purely spiritual kind is established, it always encounters the danger that everything human will be carried into and intermixed with this fellowship. A purely spiritual relationship is not only dangerous but also an altogether abnormal thing. When physical and family relationships or ordinary associations, that is, those arising from everyday life with all its claims upon people who are working together, are *not* projected into the spiritual community, then we must be especially careful. That is why, as experience has shown, it is precisely in retreats of short duration that the human element develops most easily. Nothing is easier than to stimulate the glow of fellowship in a few days of life together, but nothing is more fatal to the sound, sober, brotherly fellowship of everyday life.

There is probably no Christian to whom God has not given the uplifting *experience* of genuine Christian community at least once in his life. But in this world such experiences can be no more than a gracious extra beyond the daily bread of Christian community life. We have no claim upon such experiences, and we do not live with other Christians for the sake of acquiring them. It is not the experience of Christian brotherhood, but solid and certain faith in brotherhood that holds us together. That God has acted and wants to act upon us all, this we see in faith as

God's greatest gift, this makes us glad and happy, but it also makes us ready to forego all such experiences when God at times does not grant them. We are bound together by faith, not by experience.

'Behold, how good and how pleasant it is for brethren to dwell together in unity'—this is the Scripture's praise of life together under the Word. But now we can rightly interpret the words 'in unity' and say, 'for brethren to dwell together *through Christ*'. For Jesus Christ alone is our unity. 'He is our peace'. Through him alone do we have access to one another, joy in one another, and fellowship with one another.

II

The Day with Others

To thee our morning song of praise
To thee our evening prayer we raise;
Thy glory suppliant we adore
For ever and for evermore

AMBROSE

The Day's Beginning

'LET THE word of Christ dwell in you richly' (Col. 3.16).
The Old Testament day begins at evening and ends with the
going down of the sun. It is the time of expectation. The day
of the New Testament church begins with the break of day
and ends with the dawning light of the next morning. It is
the time of fulfilment, the resurrection of the Lord. At night
Christ was born, a light in darkness; noonday turned to night
when Christ suffered and died on the Cross. But in the dawn
of Easter morning Christ rose in victory from the grave.

Ere yet the dawn hath filled the skies
Behold my Saviour Christ arise
He chaseth from us sin and night,
And brings us joy and life and light.
Hallelujah

So sang the church of the Reformation. Christ is the 'Sun of
Righteousness', risen upon the expectant congregation
(Mal. 4.2), and they that love him shall 'be as the sun
when he goeth forth in his might' (Judg. 5.31). The early
morning belongs to the Church of the risen Christ. At the
break of light it remembers the morning on which death
and sin lay prostrate in defeat and new life and salvation
were given to mankind.

What do we today, who no longer have any fear or awe of night, know of the great joy that our forefathers and the early Christians felt every morning at the return of light? If we were to learn again something of the praise and adoration that is due the triune God at break of day, God the Father and Creator, who has preserved our life through the dark night and wakened us to a new day, God the Son and Saviour, who conquered death and hell for us, and dwells in our midst as Victor, God the Holy Spirit, who pours the bright gleam of God's Word into our hearts at the dawn of day, driving away all darkness and sin and teaching us to pray aright—then we would also begin to sense something of the joy that comes when night is past and brethren who dwell together in unity come together early in the morning for common praise of their God, common hearing of the Word, and common prayer. Morning does not belong to the individual, it belongs to the Church of the triune God, to the Christian family, to the brotherhood. Innumerable are the ancient hymns that call the congregation to common praise of God in the early morning. So the Bohemian Brethren sing at break of day:

> The day does now dark night dispel;
> Dear Christians, wake and rouse you well,
>   Give glory to God our Lord.

.   .   .   .

> Once more the daylight shines abroad,
> O brethren let us praise the Lord,
> Whose grace and mercy thus have kept
> The nightly watch while we have slept.

> We offer up ourselves to thee,
> That heart and word and deed may be
> In all things guided by thy mind,
> And in thine eyes acceptance find.

Common life under the Word begins with common worship at the beginning of the day. The family community gathers for praise and thanks, reading of the Scriptures, and prayer. The deep stillness of morning is broken first by the prayer and song of the fellowship. After the silence of night and early morning, hymns and the Word of God are more easily grasped. The Scriptures, moreover, tell us that the first thought and the first word of the day belong to God; 'My voice shalt thou hear in the morning, O Lord; in the morning will I direct my prayer unto thee' (Ps. 5.3). 'In the morning shall my prayer prevent thee' (Ps. 88.13). 'My heart is fixed, O God, my heart is fixed: I will sing and give praise. Awake up, my glory; awake, psaltery and harp; I myself will awake early' (Ps. 57.7, 8). At the dawn of day the believer thirsts and yearns for God: 'I prevented the dawning of morning, and cried: I hoped in thy word' (Ps. 119.147). 'O God, thou art my God; early will I seek thee: my soul thirsteth for thee, my flesh longeth for thee in a dry and thirsty land, where no water is' (Ps. 63.1). The Wisdom of Solomon would have it 'known that we must prevent the sun to give thee thanks, and at the dayspring pray unto thee' (16.28) and Ecclesiasticus says of the Bible student especially that 'he will give his heart to resort early to the Lord that made him and will pray before the most High' (39.5). The Bible also speaks of the morning hour as the time of God's special help. Of the city of God it is said that in the morning 'God shall help her' (Ps. 46.5); and again God's mercies 'are new every morning' (Lam. 3.23).

For Christians the beginning of the day should not be burdened and oppressed with besetting concerns for the day's work. At the threshold of the new day stands the Lord who made it. All the darkness and distraction of the dreams of night retreat before the clear light of Jesus Christ and his wakening Word. All unrest, all impurity, all care and anxiety flee before him. Therefore, at the beginning of the day let all distraction and empty talk be silenced and let the first thought and the first word belong to him to whom our whole life belongs. 'Awake thou that sleepest, and arise from the dead, and Christ shall give thee light' (Eph. 5.14).

With remarkable frequency the Scriptures remind us that the men of God rose early to seek God and carry out his commands, as did Abraham, Jacob, Moses, and Joshua (cf. Gen. 19.27, 22.3; Ex. 8.16, 9.13, 24.4; Josh. 3.1, 6.12, etc.). The Gospel, which never speaks a superfluous word, says of Jesus himself; 'And in the morning, rising up a great while before day, he went out, and departed into a solitary place, and there prayed' (Mark 1.35). Some rise early because of restlessness and worry; the Scriptures call this unprofitable : 'It is vain for you to rise up early . . . to eat the bread of sorrows' (Ps. 127.2). But there is such a thing as rising early for the love of God. This was the practice of the men of the Bible.

Common devotions in the morning should include Scripture reading, song, and prayer. Different fellowships will require different forms of worship; this is as it should be. A family with children needs a different devotion from that of a fellowship of ministers, and it is by no means wholesome for one to be like another or for a company of theologians to be content with a family devotion for children. But every common devotion should include the *word of Scripture, the hymns of the Church, and the prayer of the fellowship*. We shall speak here of these elements of common devotion.

The Secret of the Psalter

The New Testament laid emphasis upon 'speaking to yourselves in psalms' (Eph. 5.19) and 'teaching and admonishing one another in psalms' (Col. 3.16). From ancient times in the Church a special significance has been attached to the common use of psalms. In many churches to this day the Psalter constitutes the beginning of every service of common worship. The custom has been largely lost and we must find our way back to its prayers. The Psalter occupies a unique place in the Holy Scriptures. It is God's Word and, with few exceptions, the prayer of men as well. How are we to understand this? How can God's Word be at the same time prayer to God?

This question brings with it an observation that is made by everybody who begins to use the psalms as prayers. First he tries to repeat the psalms personally as his own prayer. But soon he comes upon passages that he feels he cannot utter as his own personal petitions. We recall, for example, the psalms of innocence, the bitter, the impreca- tory psalms, and also in part the psalms of the Passion. And yet these prayers are words of Holy Scripture which a believing Christian cannot simply dismiss as outworn and obsolete, as 'early stages of religion'. One may have no desire to carp at the Word of the Scriptures and yet he knows that he cannot pray these words. He can read and hear them as the prayer of another person, wonder about them, be offended by them, but he can neither pray them himself nor discard them from the Bible.

The practical expedient would be to say that any person in this situation should first stick to the psalms he can understand and repeat, and that in the case of the other psalms he should learn quite simply to let stand what is incomprehensible and difficult and turn back again and again to what is simple and understandable. Actually, how- ever, this difficulty indicates the point at which we get our first glimpse of the secret of the Psalter. A psalm we can- not utter as a prayer, that makes us falter and horrifies us, is a hint to us that here Someone else is praying, not we; that the One who is here protesting his innocence, who is invoking God's judgment, who has come to such infinite depths of suffering, is none other than Jesus Christ him- self. He it is who is praying here, and not only here but in the whole Psalter.

This insight the New Testament and the Church have always recognized and declared. The *Man* Jesus Christ, to whom no affliction, no ill, no suffering is alien and who yet was the wholly innocent and righteous one, is praying in the Psalter through the mouth of his Church. The Psalter is the prayer book of Jesus Christ in the truest sense of the word. He prayed for the Psalter and now it has become his prayer for all time. Now do we understand how the Psalter can be prayer to God and yet God's own Word, precisely because here we encounter the praying Christ? Jesus Christ prays through the Psalter in his congregation. His congregation prays too, the individual prays. But here he prays, in so far as Christ prays within him, not in his own name, but in the Name of Jesus Christ. He prays, not from the natural desires of his own heart; he prays out of the manhood put on by Christ; he prays on the basis of the prayer of the Man Jesus Christ. But when he so acts, his prayer falls within the promise that it will be heard. Because Christ prays the prayer of the psalms with the individual and the congregation before the heavenly throne of God, or rather because those who pray the psalms are joining in with the prayer of Jesus Christ, their prayer reaches the ears of God. Christ has become their inter-cessor.

The Psalter is the vicarious prayer of Christ for his Church. Now that Christ is with the Father, the new humanity of Christ, the Body of Christ on earth, continues to pray his prayer to the end of time. This prayer belongs, not to the individual member, but to the whole Body of Christ. Only in the whole Christ does the whole Psalter become a reality, a whole which the individual can never fully comprehend and call his own. That is why the prayer of the psalms belongs in a peculiar way to the fellowship. Even if a verse or a psalm is not one's own prayer, it is nevertheless the prayer of another member of the fellowship; so it is quite certainly the prayer of the true Man Jesus Christ and his Body on earth.

In the Psalter we learn to pray on the basis of Christ's prayer. The Psalter is the great school of prayer.

Here we learn, first, what prayer means. It means pray-ing according to the Word of God, on the basis of promises. Christian prayer takes its stand on the solid ground of the revealed Word and has nothing to do with vague, self-seeking vagaries. We pray on the basis of the prayer of the true Man Jesus Christ. This is what the Scripture means when it says that the Holy Spirit prays in us and for us, that Christ prays for us, that we can pray aright to God only in the name of Jesus Christ.

Second, we learn from the prayer of the psalms what we should pray. Certain as it is that the scope of the prayer of the psalms ranges far beyond the experience of the individual, nevertheless the individual prays in faith the whole prayer of Christ, the prayer of him who was true Man and who alone possesses the full range of experiences expressed in this prayer.

Can we, then, pray imprecatory psalms? In so far as we are sinners and express evil thoughts in a prayer of vengeance, we dare not do so. But in so far as Christ is in us, the Christ who took all the vengeance of God upon himself, who met God's vengeance in our stead, who thus—stricken by the wrath of God—and in no other way, could forgive his enemies, who himself suffered the wrath that his enemies might go free—we, too, as members of this Jesus Christ, can pray these psalms, through Jesus Christ, from the heart of Jesus Christ.

Can we, with the Psalmist, call ourselves innocent, devout, and righteous? We dare not do so in so far as we are ourselves. We cannot declare our virtue as the prayer of our own perverse heart. But we can and we should do so as a prayer out of the heart of Jesus Christ that was sinless and clean, out of the innocence of Christ in which he has given us a share by faith. In so far as 'Christ's blood and righteousness' has become 'our beauty, our glorious dress', we can and we should pray the psalms of innocence as Christ's prayer for us and gift to us. These psalms, too, belong to us through him.

And how shall we pray those psalms of unspeakable misery and suffering, the meaning of which we have hardly begun to sense even remotely? We can and we should pray

B

the psalms of suffering, the psalms of the passion, not in order to generate in ourselves what our hearts do not know of their own experience, not to make our own laments, but because all this suffering was real and actual in Jesus Christ, because the Man Jesus Christ suffered sickness, pain, shame, and death, because in his suffering and death all flesh suffered and died. What happened to us on the Cross of Christ, the death of our old man, and what actually does happen and should happen to us ever since our baptism in the dying of our flesh, *this* is what gives us the right to pray these prayers. Through the Cross of Christ these psalms have been bestowed upon his Body on earth as prayers that issue from his heart. We cannot enlarge upon this theme. Our concern has been only to suggest the scope and the depth of the Psalter as the prayer of Christ. Here on earth we can only grow into its meaning gradually.

Third, the psalms teach us to pray as a fellowship. The Body of Christ is praying, and as an individual one acknowledges that his prayer is only a minute fragment of the whole prayer of the Church. He learns to pray the prayer of the Body of Christ. And that lifts him above his personal concerns and allows him to pray selflessly. Many of the psalms were very probably prayed antiphonally in the Old Testament community. The so-called 'parallelism of the members', that remarkable repetition of the same sense in different words in the second line of the verse, is not merely a literary form; it also has import for the Church and theology.

It would be worth while some time to pursue this question very thoroughly. Read as a particularly clear example Psalm 5: repeatedly there are two voices, bringing the same concern to God. Is this not a hint that one who prays never prays alone? Always there must be a second person, another, a member of the fellowship, the Body of Christ, indeed, Jesus Christ himself, praying with him, in order that the prayer of the individual may be true prayer. Is there not in these repetitions of the same thought, which in Psalm 119 rise to the point where it seems that it would never end, the tremendous suggestion that every word of prayer must penetrate to a depth of the heart that can be reached only by unceasing iteration? Is this not an indication that prayer is not a matter of pouring out the human heart once and for all in need or joy, but of an unbroken, constant learning, accepting, and impressing upon the mind of God's will in Jesus Christ? Oetinger, in his exposition of the Psalms, brought out a profound truth when he arranged the whole Psalter according to the seven petitions of the Lord's Prayer. What he had discerned was that the whole sweep of the Book of Psalms was concerned with nothing more nor less than the brief petitions of the Lord's Prayer. In all our praying there remains only the prayer of Jesus Christ; this alone has the promise of fulfilment and frees us from the vain repetitions of the heathen. The more deeply we grow into the psalms and the more often we pray them as our own, the more simple and rich will our prayer become.

Reading the Scriptures

The prayer of the psalms, concluded with a hymn by the family fellowship, should be followed by a Scripture reading. 'Give attendance to reading' (I Tim. 4.13). Here, too, we shall have to overcome many harmful prejudices before we achieve the right way of reading the Scriptures together. Almost all of us have grown up with the idea that the Scripture reading is only a matter of hearing the Word of God for this particular day. That is why for many the Scripture reading consists only of a few, brief, selected verses which are to form the guiding thought of the day. There can be no doubt that the daily Bible passages published by the Moravian Brethren, for example, are a real blessing to all who have ever used them. This was discovered by many to their grateful astonishment particularly during the church struggle. But there can be equally little doubt that brief verses cannot and should not take the place of reading the Scripture as a whole. The verse for the day is still not the Holy Scripture which will remain throughout all time until the Last Day. Holy Scripture is more than a watchword. It is also more than 'light for today'. It is God's revealed Word for all men, for all times. Holy Scripture does not consist of individual passages; it is a unit and is intended to be used as such.

As a whole the Scriptures are God's revealing Word. Only in the infiniteness of its inner relationships, in the connection of Old and New Testaments, of promise and fulfilment, sacrifice and law, law and gospel, cross and resurrection, faith and obedience, having and hoping, will the full witness to Jesus Christ the Lord be perceived. This is why common devotions will include, besides the prayer of the psalms, a longer reading from the Old and the New Testament.

A Christian family fellowship should surely be able to read and listen to a chapter of the Old Testament and at least half of a chapter of the New Testament every morning and evening. When the practice is first tried, of course, most people will find even this modest measure too much and will offer resistance. It will be objected that it is impossible to take in and retain such an abundance of ideas and associations, that it even shows disrespect for God's Word to read more than one can seriously assimilate. These objections will cause us quite readily to content ourselves again with reading only verses.

In truth, however, there lurks in this attitude a grave error. If it is really true that it is hard for us, as adult Christians, to comprehend even a chapter of the Old Testament in sequence, then this can only fill us with profound shame; what kind of testimony is that to our knowledge of the Scriptures and all our previous reading of them? If we were familiar with the substance of what we read we should be able to follow a chapter without difficulty, especially if we have an open Bible in our hands and participate in the reading. But, of course, we must admit that the Scriptures are still largely unknown to us. Can the realization of our fault, our ignorance of the Word of God, have any other consequence than that we should earnestly and faithfully retrieve what has been neglected? And should not ministers be the very first to get to work at this point?

Do not object that the purpose of common devotions is profounder than to learn the contents of the Scriptures; that this is too profane a purpose, something which must be achieved apart from worship. Behind this objection there is a completely wrong understanding of what a devotion is. God's Word is to be heard by everyone in his own way and according to the measure of his understanding. A child hears and learns the Bible for the first time in family worship; the adult Christian learns it repeatedly and better, and he will never finish acquiring knowledge of its story.

Not only the young Christian but also the adult Christian will complain that the Scripture reading is often too long for him and that much therein he does not understand. To this it must be said that for the mature Christian *every* Scripture reading will be 'too long', even the shortest one. What does this mean? The Scripture is a whole and every word, every sentence, possesses such multiple relationships with the whole that it is impossible always to keep the whole in view when listening to details. It becomes apparent, therefore, that the whole of the Scripture and hence every passage in it as well far surpasses our understanding. It is good for us to be daily reminded of this fact, which again points to Jesus Christ himself, 'in whom are hid all the treasures of wisdom and knowledge' (Col. 2.3). So perhaps one may say that every Scripture reading always has to be somewhat 'too long', because it is not merely proverbial and practical wisdom but God's revealing Word in Jesus Christ.

Because the Scripture is a *corpus*, a living whole, the so-called *lectio continua* or consecutive reading must be adopted for Scripture reading in the family fellowship.

Historical books, prophets, Gospels, Epistles, and Revelation are read and heard as God's Word in their context. They set the listening fellowship in the midst of the wonderful world of revelation of the people of Israel with its prophets, judges, kings, and priests, its wars, festivals, sacrifices, and sufferings. The fellowship of believers is woven into the Christmas story, the baptism, the miracles and teaching, the suffering, dying, and rising again of Jesus Christ. It participates in the very events that occurred on this earth for the salvation of the world, and in doing so receives salvation in Jesus Christ.

Consecutive reading of biblical books forces everyone who wants to hear to put himself, or to allow himself to be found, where God has acted once and for all for the salvation of men. We become part of what once took place for our salvation. Forgetting and losing ourselves, we, too, pass through the Red Sea, through the desert, across the Jordan into the promised land. With Israel we fall into doubt and unbelief and through punishment and repentance experience again God's help and faithfulness. All this is not mere reverie but holy, godly reality. We are torn out of our own existence and set down in the midst of the holy history of God on earth. There God dealt with us, and there he still deals with us, our needs and our sins, in judgment and grace. It is not that God is the spectator and sharer of our present life, howsoever important that is; but rather that we are the reverent listeners and participants in God's action in the sacred story, the history of the Christ on earth. And only in so far as we are *there*, is God with us today also.

A complete reversal occurs. It is not in our life that God's help and presence must still be proved, but rather God's presence and help have been demonstrated for us in the life of Jesus Christ. It is in fact more important for us to know what God did to Israel, to his Son Jesus Christ, than to seek what God intends for us today. The fact that Jesus Christ died is more important than the fact that *I* shall die,

THE DAY WITH OTHERS

and the fact that Jesus Christ rose from the dead is the sole ground of my hope that I, too, shall be raised on the Last Day. Our salvation is 'external to ourselves'. I find no salvation in my life history, but only in the history of Jesus Christ. Only he who allows himself to be found in Jesus Christ, in his incarnation, his Cross, and his resurrection, is with God and God with him.

In this light the whole devotional reading of the Scriptures becomes daily more meaningful and salutary. What we call our life, our troubles, our guilt, is by no means all of reality; there in the Scriptures is our life, our need, our guilt, and our salvation. Because it pleased God to act for us there, it is only there that we shall be saved. Only in the Holy Scriptures do we learn to know our own history. The God of Abraham, Isaac, and Jacob is the God and Father of Jesus Christ and our Father.

We must learn to know the Scriptures again, as the Reformers and our fathers knew them. We must not grudge the time and the work that it takes. We must know the Scriptures first and foremost for the sake of our salvation. But besides this, there are ample reasons that make this requirement exceedingly urgent. How, for example, shall we ever attain certainty and confidence in our personal and church activity if we do not stand on solid biblical ground? It is not our heart that determines our course, but God's Word. But who in this day has any proper understanding of the need for scriptural proof? How often we hear innumerable arguments 'from life' and 'from experience' put forward as the basis for most crucial decisions, but the argument of Scripture is missing. And this authority would perhaps point in exactly the opposite direction. It is not surprising, of course, that the person who attempts to cast discredit upon their wisdom should be the one who himself does not seriously read, know, and study the Scriptures. But one who will not learn to handle the Bible for himself is not an evangelical Christian.

It might be asked further: How shall we ever help a

Christian brother and set him straight in his difficulty and doubt, if not with God's own Word? All our own words quickly fail. But he who like a good 'householder . . . bringeth forth out of his treasure things new and old' (Matt. 13.52), he who can speak out of the abundance of God's Word, the wealth of directions, admonitions, and consolations of the Scriptures, will be able through God's Word to drive out demons and help his brother. There we leave it. 'Because from childhood thou hast known the holy scriptures, they are able to instruct you unto salvation' (II Tim. 3.15, Luther's tr.).

How shall we read the Scriptures? In family devotions it is best that the various members thereof undertake the consecutive reading in turn. When this is done it will soon become apparent that it is not easy to read the Bible aloud for others. The more artless, the more objective, the more humble one's attitude toward the material is, the better will the reading accord with the subject.

Often the difference between an experienced Christian and the novice becomes clearly apparent. It may be taken as a rule for the right reading of the Scriptures that the reader should never identify himself with the person who is speaking in the Bible. It is not that I am angered, but God; it is not I giving consolation, but God; it is not I admonishing, but God admonishing in the Scriptures. I shall be able, of course, to express the fact that it is God who is angered, who is consoling and admonishing, not by indifferent monotony, but only with inmost concern and rapport, as one who knows that he himself is being addressed. It will make all the difference between right and wrong reading of Scriptures if I do not identify myself with God but quite simply serve him. Otherwise I will become rhetorical, emotional, sentimental, or coercive and imperative; that is, I will be directing the listeners' attention to myself instead of to the Word. But this is to commit the worst of sins in presenting the Scriptures.

If we may illustrate by an example in another sphere,

we might say that the situation of the reader of Scripture is probably closest to that in which I read to others a letter from a friend. I would not read that letter as though I had written it myself. The distance between us would be clearly apparent as it was read. And yet I would also be unable to read the letter of my friend to others as if it were of no concern to me. I would read it with personal interest and regard. Proper reading of Scripture is not a technical exercise that can be learned; it is something that grows or diminishes according to one's own spiritual frame of mind. The crude, ponderous rendition of the Bible by many a Christian grown old in experience often far surpasses the most highly polished reading of a minister. In a Christian family fellowship one person may give counsel and help to others in this matter also.

The consecutive reading of the Scriptures need not mean that brief Bible passages are lost. They may find their place as texts for the week or as daily verses at the beginning of devotions or for other occasions.

Singing the New Song

The prayers of the psalms and the reading of the Scriptures should be followed by the singing together of a hymn, this being the voice of the Church, praising, thanking, and praying.

'Sing unto the Lord a new song', the Psalter enjoins us again and again. It is the Christ-hymn, new every morning, that the family fellowship strikes up at the beginning of the day, the hymn that is sung by the whole Church of God on earth and in heaven, and in which we are summoned to join. God has prepared himself one great song of praise throughout eternity, and those who enter the community of God join in this song. It is the song that the 'morning stars sang together and all the sons of God shouted for joy' at the creation of the world (Job 38.7). It is the victory song of the children of Israel after passing through the Red Sea, the Magnificat of Mary after the annunciation, the song of Paul and Silas in the night of prison, the song of the singers on the sea of glass after their rescue, the 'song of Moses the servant of God, and the song of the Lamb' (Rev. 15.3). It is the new song of the heavenly fellowship.

In the morning of every day the Church on earth lifts up this song and in the evening it closes the day with this hymn. It is the triune God and his works that are extolled. This song has a different ring on earth from what it has in heaven. On earth it is the song of those who believe, in heaven the song of those who see. On earth it is a song expressed in fallible human terms, in heaven it is the 'unspeakable words, which it is not lawful for a man to utter' (II Cor. 12.4), it is the 'new song' that 'no man could learn . . . but the hundred and forty and four thousand' (Rev. 14.3), the song to which 'the harps of God' are played (Rev. 15.2).

What do we know of that new song and the harps of God? Our new song is an earthly song, a song of pilgrims and wayfarers upon whom the Word of God has dawned to light their way. Our earthly song is bound to God's revealing Word in Jesus Christ. It is the simple song of the children of this earth who have been called to be God's children; not ecstatic, not enraptured, but sober, grateful, reverent, addressed steadily to God's revealed Word.

'Sing and make melody in your heart to the Lord' (Eph. 5.19). The new song is sung first in the heart. Otherwise it cannot be sung at all. The heart sings because it is overflowing with Christ. That is why all singing in the church is a spiritual performance. Surrender to the Word, incorporation in the community, great humility, and much discipline—these are the prerequisites of all singing together. Where the heart is not singing there is no melody, there is only the dreadful medley of human self-praise. Where the singing is not to the Lord, it is singing to the honour of the self or the music, and the new song becomes a song to idols.

'Speak to yourselves in psalms and hymns and spiritual

songs' (Eph. 5.19). Our song on earth is speech. It is the sung *Word*. Why do Christians sing when they are together? The reason is quite simply, because in singing together it is possible for them to speak and pray the same Word at the same time; in other words, because here they can unite in the Word. All devotion, all attention should be concentrated upon the Word in the hymn. The fact that we do not speak it but sing it only expresses the fact that our spoken words are inadequate to express what we want to say, that the burden of our song goes far beyond all human words. Yet we do not hum a melody; we sing words of praise to God, words of thanksgiving, confession, and prayer. Thus the music is completely the servant of the Word. It elucidates the Word in its mystery.

Because it is bound wholly to the Word, the singing of the congregation, especially of the family congregation, is essentially singing in unison. Here words and music combine in a unique way. The soaring tone of unison singing finds its sole and essential support in the words that are sung and therefore does not need the musical support of other voices.

> With one voice let us sing today
> In unison both praise and pray

sang the Bohemian Brethren. 'With one mind and one mouth glorify God, even the Father of our Lord Jesus Christ' (Rom. 15.6). The purity of unison singing, unaffected by alien motives of musical techniques, the clarity, unspoiled by the attempt to give musical art an autonomy of its own apart from the words, the simplicity and frugality, the humaneness and warmth of this way of singing is the essence of all congregational singing. This, it is true, discloses itself to our cultivated ears only gradually and by patient practice. It becomes a question of a congregation's power of spiritual discernment whether it adopts proper unison singing. This is singing from the heart, singing to the Lord, singing the Word; this is singing in unity.

There are some destroyers of unison singing in the fellowship that must be rigorously eliminated. There is no place in the service of worship where vanity and bad taste can so intrude as in the singing. There is, first, the improvised second part which one hears almost everywhere. It attempts to give the necessary background, the missing fullness to the soaring unison tone, and thus kills both the words and the tone. There is the bass or the alto who must call everybody's attention to his astonishing range and therefore sings every hymn an octave lower. There is the solo voice that goes swaggering, swelling, blaring and tremulant from a full chest and drowns out everything else to the glory of its own fine organ. There are the less dangerous foes of congregational singing, the 'unmusical' who cannot sing, of whom there are far fewer than we are led to believe, and finally, there are often those also who because of some mood will not join in the singing and thus disturb the fellowship.

Unison singing, difficult as it is, is less of a musical than a spiritual matter. Only where everybody in the group is disposed to an attitude of worship and discipline can unison singing, even though it may lack much musically, give us the joy which is peculiar to it alone.

For practice in unison singing we should adopt first the Reformation chorales, then the hymns of the Bohemian Brethren and those of the ancient church. Starting here, one's judgment as to which hymns of our hymnbook lend themselves to such rendition and those which do not will be formed quite of itself. Any doctrinaire attitude, which we meet with so often in this area, comes of evil. The decision in this issue can only be made on the merits of each case, and here too we must not be iconoclastic. A Christian family fellowship will therefore try to master as large as possible a number of hymns that can be sung freely from memory. It will achieve this aim if in every devotion it includes, besides a freely selected hymn, several set stanzas that may be sung between the readings.

But there should be singing, not only at devotions, but at regular times of the day or week. The more we sing, the more joy will we derive from it, but, above all, the more devotion and discipline and joy we put into our singing, the richer will be the blessing that will come to the whole life of the fellowship from singing together.

It is the voice of the Church that is heard in singing together. It is not you that sings, it is the Church that is singing, and you, as a member of the Church, may share in its song. Thus all singing together that is right must serve to widen our spiritual horizon, make us see our little company as a member of the great Christian Church on earth, and help us willingly and gladly to join our singing, be it feeble or good, to the song of the Church.

Saying Our Prayers Together

God's Word, the voice of the Church, and our prayers belong together. So we must now speak of common prayer. 'If two of you shall agree on earth as touching any thing that they shall ask, it shall be done for them of my Father which is in heaven' (Matt. 18.19). There is no part of common devotions that raises such serious difficulties and trouble as does common prayer, for here we must ourselves begin to speak. We have heard God's Word, and we have been permitted to join in the hymn of the Church; but now we are to pray to God as a fellowship, and this prayer must really be *our* word, *our* prayer for this day, for our work, for our fellowship, for the particular needs and sins that oppress us in common, for the persons who are committed to our care.

Or should we really not pray for ourselves at all; is the desire for common prayer with our own lips and in our own words a forbidden thing? No matter what objections there may be, the fact simply remains that where Christians want to live together under the Word of God they may and they should pray together to God in their own words. They have common petitions, common thanks, common intercessions to bring to God, and they should do so joyfully and confidently. Here all fear of one another, all timidity about praying freely in one's own words in the presence of others may be put aside where in all simplicity and soberness the common, brotherly prayer is lifted to God by one of the brethren. But likewise all comment and criticism must cease whenever words of prayer howsoever halting are offered in the name of Jesus Christ. It is in fact the most normal thing in the common Christian life to pray together. Good and profitable as our restraints may be in order to keep our prayer pure and biblical, they must nevertheless not stifle necessarily free prayer itself, for Jesus Christ attached a great promise to it.

The free prayer at the close of the devotion will be said by the head of the family. But in any case it is best that it be said always by the same person, laying an unlooked-for responsibility upon this person. But in order to safeguard the prayer from being the object of the wrong kind of scrutiny and from false subjectivity, one person should pray for all over an extended period of time.

The first condition, which makes it possible for an individual to pray for the group, is the intercession of all the others for him and for his prayer. How could one person pray the prayer of the fellowship without being steadied and upheld in prayer by the fellowship itself? At this very point, every word of criticism must be transformed into fervent intercession and brotherly help. Otherwise, how easily might a fellowship be broken asunder right here!

The free prayer in the common devotion should be the prayer of the fellowship and not that of the individual who is praying. It is his responsibility to pray for the fellowship. So he will have to share the daily life of the fellowship; he must know the cares, the needs, the joys and thanksgivings, the petitions and hopes of the others. Their work and everything they bring with them must not be unknown to him. He prays as a brother among brothers. It will require practice and watchfulness, if he is not to confuse his own heart with the heart of the fellowship, if he is really to be guided solely by his responsibility to pray for the fellowship. For this reason it will be well if the person so charged is constantly given the benefit of counsel and help from others in the company, if he receives suggestions and requests to remember this or that need, or work, or even a particular person in the prayer. Thus the prayer will become more and more the common prayer of all.

Prayer, even though it be free, will be determined by a certain internal order. It is not the chaotic outburst of a human heart but the prayer of an inwardly ordered fellowship. Thus certain concerns will recur daily, even though they may perhaps appear in a different way. At first there may be some monotony in the daily recurrence of the same petitions which are required of us as a fellowship. But as time goes on there will surely come a freedom from a too individualistic accent in prayer. If it is possible to add to the number of daily recurring petitions, a weekly order or plan might be tried. If this is not possible in the common devotions, it is certainly a help in one's personal prayer times. Relating the prayer to one of the Scripture readings will also prove helpful for liberating the free prayer from the caprice of subjectivity. This gives support and substance to the prayer.

It will happen again and again that the person who is charged with offering the prayer for the fellowship will not feel at all in the spiritual mood to do so, and will much prefer to turn over his task to another for this day. Such a shift is not advisable, however. Otherwise, the prayer of the fellowship will too easily be governed by moods which have nothing to do with spiritual life. It is precisely when a person, who is borne down by inner emptiness and weariness or a sense of personal unworthiness, feels that he would like to withdraw from his task, that he should learn what it means to have a duty to perform in the fellowship, and the brethren should support him in his weakness, in his inability to pray. Perhaps it is right here that one will realize the profound truth of Paul's words: 'We know not what we should pray for as we ought: but the Spirit itself maketh intercession for us with groanings which cannot be uttered' (Rom. 8.26). Everything depends on the fellowship's understanding and supporting and praying the brother's prayer with him as its prayer.

The use of formal prayers can, under certain circumstances, be a help even for a small family group. But often a ritual becomes only an evasion of real prayer. The wealth of churchly forms and thought may easily lead us away from our own prayer; the prayers then become beautiful and profound, but not genuine. Helpful as the Church's tradition of prayer is for learning to pray, it nevertheless cannot take the place of the prayer that I owe to God this day. Here the poorest mumbling utterance can be better than the best-formulated prayer. The fact that the situation in public worship is a different one from that of daily family worship need not be explored here.

Often in the Christian community there will be a desire for special prayer fellowships beyond the daily prayers of common devotions. Here there can probably be no set rule, except one, that such meetings should be held only where there is a common desire for them and where it is certain that there will be common participation in definite hours of prayer. Any individual undertakings of this kind may well plant the seed of destruction in the community. It is precisely in this area that there must be a demonstration of the strong bearing the burdens of the weak, and of the weak not judging the strong. The New Testament teaches us that a free prayer fellowship is the most natural thing in Christian practice and may be viewed without suspicion. But where there is mistrust and uneasiness, one must bear the other in patience. Let nothing be done by force; let everything be done in freedom and love.

The Fellowship of the Table

We have been following the course of the Christian community's morning worship. God's Word, the hymn of the Church and the prayer of the fellowship stand at the threshold of the day. Not until the fellowship has been nourished and strengthened with the bread of eternal life does it come together to receive from God earthly bread for this temporal life. Giving thanks and asking God's blessing, the Christian family receives its daily bread from the hand of the Lord. Ever since Jesus Christ sat at table with his disciples, the table fellowship of his community has been blessed with his presence. 'And it came to pass, as he sat at meat with them, he took bread, and blessed it, and brake, and gave to them. And their eyes were opened, and they knew him' (Luke 24.30-31).

The Scriptures speak of three kinds of table fellowship that Jesus keeps with his own : daily fellowship at table, the table fellowship of the Lord's Supper, and the final table fellowship in the Kingdom of God. But in all three the one thing that counts is that 'their eyes were opened, and they knew him'.

To know Jesus Christ in the presence of these gifts— what does this mean

It means, first, to know him as the giver of all gifts, as the Lord and Creator of this our world, with the Father and the Holy Spirit. The table fellowship therefore prays, 'And let *thy* gifts to us be blest', and thus acknowledges the eternal divinity of Jesus Christ.

Second, the fellowship acknowledges that all earthly gifts are given to it only for Christ's sake, as this whole world is sustained only for the sake of Jesus Christ, his Word, and his message. He is the true bread of life. He is not only the giver but the gift itself, for whose sake all earthly gifts exist. Only because the message concerning Jesus Christ must still go forth and find believers, and because our task is not yet perfected, does God in his patience continue to sustain us with his good gifts. So the Christian table fellowship prays, in Luther's words : 'O Lord God, heavenly Father, bless unto us these thy gifts, which of thy tender kindness thou hast bestowed upon us, through *Jesus Christ our Lord*. Amen', thus confessing that Jesus Christ is the divine Mediator and Saviour.

Third, the congregation of Jesus believes that its Lord wills to be present when it prays for his presence. So it prays: 'Come, Lord Jesus, be our guest'—and thereby confesses the gracious omnipresence of Jesus Christ. Every mealtime fills Christians with gratitude for the living, present Lord and God, Jesus Christ. Not that they seek any morbid spiritualization of material gifts; on the contrary, Christians, in their wholehearted joy in the good gifts of this physical life, acknowledge their Lord as the true giver of all good gifts; and beyond this, as the true Gift; the true Bread of life itself; and finally, as the One who is calling them to the banquet of the Kingdom of God. So in a singular way, the daily table fellowship binds the Christians to their Lord and one another. At table they know their Lord as the one who breaks bread for them; the eyes of their faith are opened.

The fellowship of the table has a festive quality. It is a constantly recurring reminder in the midst of our everyday work of God's resting after his work, of the Sabbath as the meaning and goal of the week and its toil. Our life is not only travail and labour, it is also refreshment and joy in the goodness of God. We labour, but God nourishes and sustains us. And this is the reason for celebrating. Man should not eat the bread of sorrows (Ps. 127.2); rather 'eat thy bread with joy' (Eccl. 9.7); 'I commended mirth, because a man hath no better thing under the sun, than to eat, and to drink, and to be merry' (8.15); but, of course, 'who can eat, or who can have enjoyment apart from him?' (2.25, A.R.V.). It is said of the seventy elders of Israel who went up to Mount Sinai with Moses and Aaron that 'they beheld God and did eat and drink' (Ex. 24.11, A.R.V.). God cannot endure that unfestive, mirthless attitude of ours in which we eat our bread in sorrow, with pretentious, busy haste, or even with shame. Through our daily meals he is calling us to rejoice, to keep holiday in the midst of our working day.

The table fellowship of Christians implies obligation. It is *our* daily bread that we eat, not my own. We share our bread. Thus we are firmly bound to one another not only in the Spirit but in our whole physical being. The *one* bread that is given to our fellowship links us together in a firm covenant. Now none dares go hungry as long as another has bread, and he who breaks this fellowship of the physical life also breaks the fellowship of the Spirit. 'Deal thy bread to the hungry' (Isa. 58.7). 'Make not a hungry soul sorrowful' (Ecclus. 4.2), for the Lord is meeting us in the hungry (Matt. 25.37). 'If a brother or a sister be naked, and destitute of daily food, and one of you say unto them, Depart in peace, be ye warmed and filled; notwithstanding ye give them not those things which are needful of the body, what doth it profit?' (James, 2.15, 16). So long as we eat our bread together we shall have sufficient even with the least. Not until one person desires to keep his own bread for himself does hunger ensue. This is a strange divine law. May not the story of the miraculous feeding of the five thousand with two fishes and five loaves have, along with many others, this meaning also?

The fellowship of the table teaches Christians that here they still eat the perishable bread of the earthly pilgrimage. But if they share this bread with one another, they shall also one day receive the imperishable bread together in the Father's house. 'Blessed is he that shall eat bread in the kingdom of God' (Luke 14.15).

The Day's Work

After the first morning hour the Christian's day until evening belongs to work. 'Man goeth forth unto his work and to his labour until the evening' (Ps. 104.23). In most cases the Christian family fellowship will separate for the duration of the working day. Praying and working are two different things. Prayer should not be hindered by work, but neither should work be hindered by prayer. Just as it was God's will that man should work six days and rest and make holy day in his presence on the seventh, so it is also God's will that every day should be marked for the Christian by both prayer and work. Prayer is entitled to its time. But the bulk of the day belongs to work. And only where each receives its own specific due will it become clear that both belong inseparably together. Without the burden and labour of the day, prayer is not prayer, and without prayer work is not work. This only the Christian knows. Thus, it is precisely in the clear distinction between them that their oneness becomes manifest.

Work plunges men into the world of things. The Christian steps out of the world of brotherly encounter into the world of impersonal things, the 'it'; and this new encounter frees him for objectivity; for the 'it'-world is only an instrument in the hand of God for the purification of Christians from all self-centredness and self-seeking. The work of the world can be done only where a person forgets himself, where he loses himself in a cause, in reality, the task, the 'it'. In work the Christian learns to allow himself to be limited by the task, and thus for him the work becomes a remedy against the indolence and sloth of the flesh. The passions of the flesh die in the world of things. But this can happen only where the Christian breaks through the 'it' to the 'Thou', which is God, who bids him work and makes that work a means of liberation from himself.

The work does not cease to be work; on the contrary, the hardness and rigour of labour is really sought only by the one who knows what it does for him. The continuing struggle with the 'it' remains. But at the same time the break-through is made; the unity of prayer and work, the unity of the day is discovered; for to find, behind the 'it' of the day's work, the 'Thou', which is God, is what Paul calls 'praying without ceasing' (I Thess. 5.17). Thus the prayer of the Christian reaches beyond its set time and extends into the heart of his work. It includes the whole day, and in doing so, it does not hinder the work; it promotes it, affirms it, and lends it meaning and joy. Thus every word, every work, every labour of the Christian becomes a prayer; not in the unreal sense of a constant turning away from the task that must be done, but in a real breaking through the hard 'it' to the gracious Thou. 'Whatsoever ye do in word or deed, do all in the name of the Lord Jesus' (Col. 3.17).

Then from this achieved unity of the day the whole day acquires an order and a discipline. These must be sought and found in the morning prayer and in work they will be maintained. The prayer of the morning will determine the day. Wasted time, which we are ashamed of, temptations that beset us, weakness and listlessness in our work, disorder and indiscipline in our thinking and our relations with other people, very frequently have their cause in neglect of the morning prayer. The organization and distribution of our time will be better for having been rooted in prayer. The temptations which the working day brings with it will be overcome by this break-through to God. Decisions which our work demands will be simpler and easier when they are made, not in the fear of men, but solely in the presence of God. 'Whatsoever ye do, do it heartily, as to the Lord, and not unto men' (Col. 3.23). Even routine mechanical work will be performed more patiently when it is done with the knowledge of God and his command. Our strength and energy for work increase when we have prayed to God to give us the strength we need for our daily work.

Noonday and Evening

The noonday hour, where it is possible, becomes for the Christian family fellowship a brief rest on the day's march. Half of the day is past. The fellowship thanks God and prays for protection until the eventide. It receives its daily bread and prays, in the words of the Reformation hymn :

Feed us, O Father, thy children,
Comfort us, afflicted sinners.

God must feed us. We cannot and dare not demand this
food as our right, for we, poor sinners, have not merited it.
Thus the sustenance that God provides becomes a consolation of the afflicted; for it is the token of the grace and
faithfulness with which God supports and guides his children. True, the Scriptures say, 'If any will not work,
neither let him eat' (II Thess. 3.10, A.R.V.), and thus make
the receiving of bread strictly dependent upon working for
it. But the Scriptures do not say anything about any claim
that the working person has upon God for his bread. The
work is commanded, indeed, but the bread is God's free
and gracious gift. We cannot simply take it for granted
that our work provides us with bread; this is rather God's
order of grace.

To him alone the day belongs, and so, in the middle of
the day, the Christian fellowship gathers and accepts God's
invitation to come and eat. Noon is one of the seven prayer
hours of the Church and the Psalmist. At the height of the
day the Church lifts up its voice to the triune God in praise
of his wonders and prayer for help and speedy redemption.
At midday the heavens were darkened above the Cross of
Jesus. The work of atonement was approaching its com-
pletion. And where a Christian family fellowship is able to
gather together at this hour for a brief devotion of song
and prayer, it will not do so in vain.

The labour of the day comes to its end. When the day has
been hard and toilsome, the Christian will understand
what Paul Gerhardt meant when he said:

My head and hands and feet
Their rest with gladness greet,
    And know their work is o'er;
My heart, thou too shalt be
From sinful works set free,
    Nor pine in weary sorrow more.

A day at a time is long enough to sustain one's faith; the next day will have its own cares.

Again the Christian family gathers together. The fellowship is united at the evening table and the last devotion. With the disciples in Emmaus they pray: 'Abide with us: for it is toward evening, and the day is far spent' (Luke 24.29). It is an excellent thing if the evening devotion can be held at the actual end of the day, thus becoming the last word before the night's rest. When night falls, the true light of God's Word shines brighter for the Church. The prayer of the Psalms, a hymn, and common prayer close the day, as they opened it.

We have yet to say a few words with regard to evening prayer. This is the appropriate place for common intercessions. After the day's work we pray God for the blessing, peace, and safety of all Christendom; for our congregation; for the pastor in his ministry; for the poor, the wretched, and lonely; for the sick and dying; for our neighbours, for our own folks at home, and for our fellowship. When can we have any deeper sense of God's power and working than in the hour when our hands lay down their work and we commit ourselves to the hands of God? When are we more ready for the prayer of blessing, peace, and preservation than the time when our own activity ceases? When we grow weary, God does his work. 'Behold he that keepeth Israel shall neither slumber nor sleep' (Ps. 121.4).

Then, too, the evening prayer of the family fellowship should include particularly the petition of forgiveness for every wrong done to God and our brothers, for God's forgiveness and that of our brothers, and for readiness gladly to forgive any wrong done to us. It is an ancient monastic custom that by fixed order in the evening devotions the abbot begs the forgiveness of the brothers for all faults and defaults committed against them, and after the brothers assure him of their forgiveness they likewise beg the abbot's forgiveness of their faults and defaults and receive his forgiveness. 'Let not the sun go down on your wrath'

(Eph. 4.26). It is a decisive rule of every Christian fellow-ship that every dissension that the day has brought must be healed in the evening. It is perilous for the Christian to lie down to sleep with an unreconciled heart. Therefore, it is well that there be a special place for the prayer of brotherly forgiveness in every evening's devotion, that re-conciliation be made and fellowship established anew.

Finally, in all the ancient evening prayers we are struck by the frequency with which we encounter the prayer for preservation during the night from the devil, from terror, and from an evil, sudden death. The ancients had a per-sistent sense of a man's helplessness while sleeping, of the kinship of sleep with death, of the devil's cunning in making a man fall when he is defenceless. So they prayed for the protection of the holy angels and their golden weapons, for the heavenly hosts, at the time when Satan would gain power over them. Most remarkable and pro-found is the ancient church's prayer that when our eyes are closed in sleep God may nevertheless keep our hearts awake. It is the prayer that God may dwell with us and in us even though we are unconscious of his presence, that he may keep our hearts pure and holy in spite of all the cares and temptations of the night, to make our hearts ever alert to hear his call and, like the boy Samuel, answer him even in the night: 'Speak, Lord; for thy servant heareth' (I Sam. 3.9). Even in sleep we are in the hands of God or in the power of evil. Even in sleep God can perform his wonders upon us or evil bring us to destruction. So we pray at evening:

> When our eyes with sleep are girt,
> Be our hearts to thee alert;
> Shield us, Lord, with thy right arm,
> Save us from sin's dreadful harm.
>
> LUTHER

But over the night and over the day stands the word of the Psalter: 'The day is thine, the night also is thine' (Ps. 74.16).

III

The Day Alone

MANY PEOPLE seek fellowship because they are afraid to be alone. Because they cannot stand loneliness, they are driven to seek the company of other people. There are Christians, too, who cannot endure being alone, who have had some bad experiences with themselves, who hope they will gain some help in association with others. They are generally disappointed. Then they blame the fellowship for what is really their own fault. The Christian community is not a spiritual sanatorium. The person who comes into a fellowship because he is running away from himself is misusing it for the sake of diversion, no matter how spiritual this diversion may appear. He is really not seeking community at all, but only distraction which will allow him to forget his loneliness for a brief time, the very alienation that creates the deadly isolation of man The disintegration of communication and all genuine experience, and finally resignation and spiritual death are the result of such attempts to find a cure.

Solitude and Silence

Let him who cannot be alone beware of community. He will only do harm to himself and to the community. Alone you stood before God when he called you; alone you had to answer that call; alone you had to struggle and pray; and alone you will die and give an account to God. You cannot escape from yourself; for God has singled you out. If you refuse to be alone you are rejecting Christ's call to you, and you can have no part in the community of those who are called. 'The challenge of death comes to us all, and no one can die for another. Everyone must fight his own battle with death by himself, alone. . . . I will not be with you then, nor you with me' (Luther).

But the reverse is also true : *Let him who is not in community beware of being alone.* Into the community you were called, the call was not meant for you alone; in the community of the called you bear your cross, you struggle, you pray. You are not alone, even in death, and on the Last Day you will be only one member of the great congregation of Jesus Christ. If you scorn the fellowship of the brethren, you reject the call of Jesus Christ, and thus your solitude can only be hurtful to you. 'If I die, then I am not alone in death; if I suffer they [the fellowship] suffer with me' (Luther).

We recognize, then, that only as we are within the fellowship can we be alone, and only he that is alone can live in the fellowship. Only in the fellowship do we learn to be rightly alone and only in aloneness do we learn to live rightly in the fellowship. It is not as though the one preceded the other; both begin at the same time, namely, with the call of Jesus Christ.

Each by itself has profound pitfalls and perils. One who wants fellowship without solitude plunges into the void of words and feelings, and one who seeks solitude without fellowship perishes in the abyss of vanity, self-infatuation, and despair.

Let him who cannot be alone beware of community. Let him who is not in community beware of being alone.

Along with the day of the Christian family fellowship together there goes the lonely day of the individual. This is as it should be. The day together will be unfruitful without the day alone, both for the fellowship and for the individual.

The mark of solitude is silence, as speech is the mark of community. Silence and speech have the same inner correspondence and difference as do solitude and community. One does not exist without the other. Right speech comes out of silence, and right silence comes out of speech.

Silence does not mean dumbness, as speech does not mean chatter. Dumbness does not create solitude and chatter does not create fellowship. 'Silence is the excess, the inebriation, the victim of speech. But dumbness is unholy, like a thing only maimed, not cleanly sacrificed. . . . Zacharias was speechless, instead of being silent. Had he accepted the revelation, he may perhaps have come out of the temple not dumb but silent' (Ernest Hello). The speech, the Word which establishes and binds together the fellowship, is accompanied by silence. 'There is a time to keep silence and a time to speak' (Eccl. 3.7). As there are definite hours in the Christian's day for the Word, particularly the time of common worship and prayer, so the day also needs definite times of silence, silence under the Word and silence that comes out of the Word. These will be especially the times before and after hearing the Word. The Word comes not to the chatterer but to him who holds his tongue. The stillness of the temple is the sign of the holy presence of God in his Word.

There is an indifferent, or even negative, attitude toward silence which sees in it a disparagement of God's revelation in the Word. This is the view which misinterprets silence as a ceremonial gesture, as a mystical desire to get beyond the Word. This is to miss the essential relationship of silence to the Word. Silence is the simple stillness of the individual under the Word of God. We are silent before hearing the Word because our thoughts are already directed to the Word, as a child is quiet when he enters his father's room. We are silent after hearing the Word because the Word is still speaking and dwelling within us. We are silent at the beginning of the day because God should have the first word, and we are silent before going to sleep because the last word also belongs to God. We keep silence solely for the sake of the Word, and therefore not in order to show disregard for the Word but rather to honour and receive it.

Silence is nothing else but waiting for God's Word and coming from God's Word with a blessing. But everybody knows that this is something that needs to be practised and learned, in these days when talkativeness prevails. Real silence, real stillness, really holding one's tongue comes only as the sober consequence of spiritual stillness.

But this stillness before the Word will exert its influence upon the whole day. If we have learned to be silent before the Word, we shall also learn to manage our silence and our speech during the day. There is such a thing as forbidden, self-indulgent silence, a proud, offensive silence. And this means that it can never be merely silence as such. The silence of the Christian is listening silence, humble stillness, that may be interrupted at any time for the sake of humility. It is silence in conjunction with the Word. This is what Thomas à Kempis meant when he said: 'None speaketh surely but he that would gladly keep silence if he might.' There is a wonderful power of clarification, purification, and concentration upon the essential thing in being quiet. This is true as a purely secular fact. But silence before the Word leads to right hearing and thus also to right speaking of the Word of God at the right time. Much that is unnecessary remains unsaid. But the essential and the helpful thing can be said in a few words.

Where a family lives close together in a constricted space and the individual does not have the quietness he needs, regular times of quiet are absolutely necessary. After a time of quiet we meet others in a different and a fresh way. Many a household fellowship will be able to provide for the individual's need to be alone, and thus preserve the fellowship itself from injury, only by adopting a regular order.

We shall not discuss here all the wonderful benefits that can accrue to the Christian in solitude and silence. It is all too easy to go astray at this point. We could probably cite many a bad experience that has come from silence. Silence can be a dreadful ordeal with all its desolation and terrors. It can also be a false paradise of self-deception; the latter is no better than the former. Be that as it may, let none expect from silence anything but a direct encounter with the Word of God, for the sake of which he has entered into silence. But this encounter will be given to him. The Christian will not lay down any conditions as to what he expects or hopes to get from this encounter. If he will simply accept it, his silence will be richly rewarded.

There are three purposes for which the Christian needs a definite time when he can be alone during the day: Scripture meditation, prayer, and intercession. All three should have their place in the daily period of meditation. The word 'meditation' should not frighten us. It is an ancient concept of the Church and of the Reformation that we are beginning again to rediscover.

Meditation

It might be asked, Why is a special time needed for this, since we meditate already during the common devotions?

This is the answer. The period of personal meditation is to be devoted to the Scriptures, private prayer, and intercession, and it has no other purpose. There is no occasion here for spiritual experiments. But for these three things there must be time, for God himself requires them of us. Even if initially meditation means nothing but this one thing, that we are performing a service that we owe to God, it would still be sufficient.

The time of meditation does not let us down into the void and abyss of loneliness; it lets us be alone with the Word. And in doing so it gives us solid ground on which to stand and clear directions as to the steps we must take.

Whereas in our devotions together we read long consecutive passages, in our personal meditation we confine ourselves to a brief selected text, which possibly may not be changed for a whole week. If in our reading of the Scriptures together we are led into the whole length and breadth of the Bible, here we go into the unfathomable depths of a particular sentence and word. Both are equally necessary, 'that ye may be able to comprehend with all saints what is the breadth, and length, and depth, and height' (Eph. 3.18).

In our meditation we ponder the chosen text on the strength of the promise that it has something utterly personal to say to us for this day and for our Christian life, that it is not only God's Word for the Church, but also God's Word for us individually. We expose ourselves to the specific word until it addresses us personally. And when we do this, we are doing no more than the simplest, untutored Christian does every day; we read God's Word as God's Word for us.

We do not ask what this text has to say to other people. For the preacher this means that he will not ask how he is going to preach or teach on this text, but what it is saying quite directly to him. It is true that to do this we must first have understood the content of the verse, but here we are not expounding it or preparing a sermon or conducting Bible study of any kind; we are rather waiting for God's Word to us. It is not a vacuous waiting, but a waiting on the basis of a clear promise. Often we are so burdened and overwhelmed with other thoughts, images, and concerns that it may take a long time before God's Word has swept all else aside and come through. But it will surely come, just as surely as God himself has come to men and will come again. This is the very reason why we begin our meditation with the prayer that God may send his Holy Spirit to us through his Word and reveal his Word to us and enlighten us.

It is not necessary that we should get through the entire passage in one meditation. Often we shall have to stop with one sentence or even one word, because we have been gripped and arrested and cannot evade it any longer. Is not the word 'Father', or 'love', 'mercy', 'cross', 'sanctification', 'resurrection', often enough to fill far more than the brief period we have at our disposal?

It is not necessary, therefore, that we should be concerned in our meditation to express our thought and prayer in words. Unphrased thought and prayer, which issues only from our hearing, may often be more beneficial.

It is not necessary that we should discover new ideas in our meditation. Often this only diverts us and feeds our vanity. It is sufficient if the Word, as we read and understand it, penetrates and dwells within us. As Mary 'pondered in her heart' the things that were told by the shepherds, as what we have casually overheard follows us for a long time, sticks in our mind, occupies, disturbs, or delights us, without our ability to do anything about it, so in meditation God's Word seeks to enter in and remain with us. It strives to stir us, to work and operate in us, so that we shall not get away from it the whole day long. Then it will do its work in us, without our being conscious of it.

Above all, it is not necessary that we should have any unexpected, extraordinary experiences in meditation. This can happen, but if it does not, it is not a sign that the meditation period has been useless. Not only at the beginning, but repeatedly, there will be times when we feel a great spiritual dryness and apathy, an aversion, even inability to meditate. We dare not be balked by such experiences. Above all, we must not allow them to keep us from adhering to our meditation period with great patience and fidelity.

It is, therefore, not good for us to take too seriously the many untoward experiences we have with ourselves in meditation. It is here that our old vanity and our illicit claims upon God may creep in by a pious detour, as if it were our right to have nothing but elevating and fruitful experiences, and as if the discovery of our own inner poverty were quite below our dignity. With that attitude we shall make no progress. Impatience and self-reproach will only foster our complacency and entangle us ever more deeply in the net of self-centred introspection. But there is no more time for such morbidity in meditation than there is in the Christian life as a whole. We must centre our attention on the Word alone and leave consequences to its action. For may it not be that God himself sends us these hours of reproof and dryness that we may be brought again to expect everything from his Word? 'Seek God, not happiness'—this is the fundamental rule of all meditation. If you seek God alone, you will gain happiness: that is its promise.

Prayer

The Scripture meditation leads to prayer. We have already said that the most promising method of prayer is to allow oneself to be guided by the word of the Scriptures, to pray on the basis of a word of Scripture. In this way we shall not become the victims of our own emptiness. Prayer means nothing else but the readiness and willingness to receive and appropriate the Word, and, what is more, to accept in one's personal situation, particular tasks, decisions, sins, and temptations. What can never enter the corporate prayer of the fellowship may here be silently made known to God. According to a word of Scripture we pray for the clarification of our day, for preservation from sin, for growth in sanctification, for faithfulness and strength in our work. And we may be certain that our prayer will be heard, because it is a response to God's Word and promise. Because God's Word has found its fulfilment in Jesus Christ, all prayers that we pray conforming to this Word are certainly heard and answered in Jesus Christ.

It is one of the particular difficulties of meditation that our thoughts are likely to wander and go their own way, toward other persons or to some events in our life. Much as this may distress and shame us again and again, we must not lose heart and become anxious, or even conclude that meditation is really not something for us. When this happens it is often a help not to snatch back our thoughts convulsively, but quite calmly to incorporate into our prayer the people and events to which our thoughts keep straying and thus in all patience return to the starting point of the meditation.

Intercession

Just as we relate our personal prayer to the Scripture passage so we do the same with our intercessions. It is impossible to mention in the intercessions of corporate worship all the persons who are committed to our care, or at any rate to do so in the way that is required of us. Every Christian has his own circle who have requested him to make intercession for them or for whom he knows he has been called upon especially to pray. These will be, first of all, those with whom he must live day by day.

This brings us to a point at which we hear the pulsing heart of all Christian life in unison. A Christian fellowship lives and exists by the intercession of its members for one another, or it collapses. I can no longer condemn or hate a brother for whom I pray, no matter how much trouble he causes me. His face, that hitherto may have been strange and intolerable to me, is transformed in intercession into the countenance of a brother for whom Christ died, the face of a forgiven sinner. This is a happy discovery for the Christian who begins to pray for others. There is no dislike, no personal tension, no estrangement that cannot be overcome by intercession as far as our side of it is concerned. Intercessory prayer is the purifying bath into which the individual and the fellowship must enter every day. The struggle we undergo with our brother in intercession may be a hard one, but that struggle has the promise that it will gain its goal.

How does this happen? Intercession means no more than to bring our brother into the presence of God, to see him under the Cross of Jesus as a poor human being and sinner in need of grace. Then everything in him that repels us falls away; and we see him in all his destitution and need. His

C

need and his sin become so heavy and oppressive that we feel them as our own, and we can do nothing else but pray: Lord, do thou, thou alone, deal with him according to thy severity and thy goodness. To make intercession means to grant our brother the same right that we have received, namely, to stand before Christ and share in his mercy.

This makes it clear that intercession is also a daily service we owe to God and our brother. He who denies his neighbour the service of praying for him denies him the service of a Christian. It is clear, furthermore, that intercession is not general and vague but very concrete: a matter of definite persons and definite difficulties and therefore of definite petitions. The more definite my intercession becomes, the more promising it is.

Finally, we can also no longer escape the realization that the ministry of intercession requires time of every Christian, but most of all of the pastor who has the responsibility of a whole congregation. Intercession alone, if it is thoroughly done, would consume the entire time of daily meditation. So pursued, it will become evident that intercession is a gift of God's grace for every Christian community and for every Christian. Because intercession is such an incalculably great gift of God, we should accept it joyfully. The very time we give to intercession will turn out to be a daily source of new joy in God and in the Christian community.

Since meditation on the Scriptures, prayer, and intercession are a service we owe and because the grace of God is found in this service, we should train ourselves to set apart a regular hour for it, as we do for every other service we perform. This is not 'legalism'; it is orderliness and fidelity. For most people the early morning will prove to be the best time. We have a right to this time, even prior to the claims of other people, and we may insist upon having it as a completely undisturbed quiet time despite all external difficulties. For the pastor it is an indispensable duty and his whole ministry will depend on it. Who can really be faithful in great things if he has not learned to be faithful in the things of daily life?

The Test of Meditation

testing

Every day brings to the Christian many hours in which he will be alone in an unchristian environment. These are the times of *testing*. This is the test of true meditation and true Christian community. Has the fellowship served to make the individual free, strong, and mature, or has it made him weak and dependent? Has it taken him by the hand for a while in order that he may learn again to walk by himself, or has it made him uneasy and unsure? This is one of the most searching and critical questions that can be put to any Christian fellowship.

Furthermore, this is the place where we find out whether the Christian's meditation has led him into the unreal, from which he awakens in terror when he returns to the work-aday world, or whether it has led him into a real contact with God, from which he emerges strengthened and purified. Has it transported him for a moment into a spiritual ecstasy that vanishes when everyday life returns, or has it lodged the Word of God so securely and deeply in his heart that it holds and fortifies him, impelling him to active love, to obedience, to good works? Only the day can decide.

Is the invisible presence of the Christian fellowship a reality and a help to the individual? Do the intercessions of others carry him through the day? Is the Word of God close to him as a comfort and a strength? Or does he misuse his aloneness contrary to the fellowship, the Word, and the prayer? The individual must realize that his hours of aloneness react upon the community. In his solitude he can sunder and besmirch the fellowship, or he can strengthen and hallow it. Every act of self-control of the Christian is also a service to the fellowship.

On the other hand, there is no sin in thought, word, or deed, no matter how personal or secret, that does not inflict injury upon the whole fellowship. An element of sickness gets into the body; perhaps nobody knows where it comes from or in what member it has lodged, but the body is infected. This is the proper metaphor for the Christian community. We *are* members of a body, not only when we choose to be, but in our whole existence. Every member serves the whole body, either to its health or to its destruction. This is no mere theory; it is a spiritual reality. And the Christian community has often experienced its effects with disturbing clarity, sometimes destructively and sometimes fortunately.

One who returns to the Christian family fellowship after fighting the battle of the day brings with him the blessing of his aloneness, but he himself receives anew the blessing of the fellowship. Blessed is he who is alone in the strength of the fellowship and blessed is he who keeps the fellowship in the strength of aloneness. But the strength of aloneness and the strength of the fellowship is solely the strength of the Word of God, which is addressed to the individual in the fellowship.

IV

Ministry

'THERE AROSE a reasoning among them, which of them should be the greatest' (Luke 9.46). We know who it is that sows this thought in the Christian community. But perhaps we do not bear in mind enough that no Christian community ever comes together without this thought immediately emerging as a seed of discord. Thus at the very beginning of Christian fellowship there is engendered an invisible, often unconscious, life-and-death contest. 'There arose a reasoning among them': this is enough to destroy a fellowship.

Hence it is vitally necessary that every Christian community from the very outset face this dangerous enemy squarely, and eradicate it. There is no time to lose here, for from the first moment when a man meets another person he is looking for a strategic position he can assume and hold over against that person. There are strong persons and weak ones. If a man is not strong, he immediately claims the right of the weak as his own and uses it against the strong. There are gifted and ungifted persons, simple people and difficult people, devout and less devout, the sociable and the solitary. Does not the ungifted person have to take up a position just as well as the gifted person, the difficult one as well as the simple? And if I am not gifted, then perhaps I am devout anyhow; or if I am not devout it is only because I do not want to be. May not the sociable individual carry the field before him and put the timid, solitary man to shame? Then may not the solitary person become the undying enemy and ultimate vanquisher of his sociable adversary? Where is there a person who does not with

instinctive sureness find the spot where he can stand and
defend himself, but which he will never give up to another,
for which he will fight with all the drive of his instinct
of self-assertion?

All this can occur in the most polite or even pious environment. But the important thing is that a Christian
community should know that somewhere in it there will
certainly be 'a reasoning among them, which of them
should be the greatest.' It is the struggle of the natural
man for self-justification. He finds it only in comparing
himself with others, in condemning and judging others.
Self-justification and judging others go together, as justification by grace and serving others go together.

The Ministry of Holding One's Tongue

Often we combat our evil thoughts most effectively if we
absolutely refuse to allow them to be expressed in words.
It is certain that the spirit of self-justification can be overcome only by the Spirit of grace; nevertheless, isolated
thoughts of judgment can be curbed and smothered by
never allowing them the right to be uttered, except as a
confession of sin, which we shall discuss later. He who
holds his tongue in check controls both mind and body
(James 3.2ff.). Thus it must be a decisive rule of every
Christian fellowship that each individual is prohibited from
saying much that occurs to him. This prohibition does not
include the personal word of advice and guidance: on this
point we shall speak later. But to speak about a brother
covertly is forbidden, even under the cloak of help and
good will; for it is precisely in this guise that the spirit of
hatred among brothers always creeps in when it is seeking
to create mischief.

This is not the place to discuss the limitations upon this
rule in particular cases. They must be a matter of decision
in each instance. The point, however, is clear and biblical:

'Thou sittest and speakest against thy brother: thou
slanderest thine own mother's son. These things hast thou

done, and I kept silence; thou thoughtest that I was altogether such an one as thyself: but I will reprove thee, and set them in order before thine eyes' (Ps. 50.20-21).

'Speak not evil one of another, brethren. He that speaketh evil of his brother, and judgeth his brother, speaketh evil of the law, and judgeth the law: but if thou judge the law, thou art not a doer of the law, but a judge. There is one lawgiver, who is able to save and to destroy: who art thou that judgest another?' (James 4.11-12).

'Let no corrupt communication proceed out of your mouth, but that which is good to the use of edifying, that it may minister grace unto the hearers' (Eph. 4.29).

Where this discipline of the tongue is practised right from the beginning, each individual will make a matchless discovery. He will be able to cease from constantly scrutinizing the other person, judging him, condemning him, putting him in his particular place where he can gain ascendancy over him and thus doing violence to him as a person. Now he can allow the brother to exist as a completely free person, as God made him to be. His view expands and, to his amazement, for the first time he sees, shining above his brethren, the richness of God's creative glory. God did not make this person as I would have made him. He did not give him to me as a brother for me to dominate and control, but in order that I might find above him the Creator. Now the other person, in the freedom with which he was created, becomes the occasion of joy, whereas before he was only a nuisance and an affliction. God does not will that I should fashion the other person according to the image that seems good to me, that is, in my own image; rather in his very freedom from me God made this person in his image. I can never know beforehand how God's image should appear in others. That image always manifests a completely new and unique form that comes solely from God's free and sovereign creation. To me the sight may seem strange, even ungodly. But God creates every man in the likeness of his Son, the Crucified. After all, even that image certainly looked strange and ungodly to me before I grasped it.

Strong and weak, wise and foolish, gifted or ungifted, pious or impious, the diverse individuals in the community are no longer incentives for talking and judging and condemning, and thus excuses for self-justification. They are rather cause for rejoicing in one another and serving one another. Each member of the community is given his particular place, but this is no longer the place in which he can most successfully assert himself, but the place where he can best perform his service.

In a Christian community everything depends upon whether each individual is an indispensable link in a chain. Only when even the smallest link is securely interlocked is the chain unbreakable. A community which allows unemployed members to exist within it will perish because of them. It will be well, therefore, if every member receives a definite task to perform for the community, that he may know in hours of doubt that he, too, is not useless and unusable. Every Christian community must realize that not only do the weak need the strong, but also that the strong cannot exist without the weak. The elimination of the weak is the death of the fellowship.

Not self-justification, which means the use of domination and force, but justification by grace, and therefore service, should govern the Christian community. Once a man has experienced the mercy of God in his life he will henceforth aspire only to serve. The proud throne of the judge no longer lures him; he wants to be down below with the lowly and the needy, because that is where God found him. 'Mind not high things, but condescend to men of low estate' (Rom. 12.16).

The Ministry of Meekness

He who would learn to serve must first learn to think little of himself. Let no man 'think of himself more highly than he ought to think' (Rom. 12.3). 'This is the highest and most profitable lesson, truly to know and to despise ourselves. To have no opinion of ourselves, and to think always well and highly of others, is great wisdom and perfection' (Thomas à Kempis). 'Be not wise in your own conceits' (Rom. 12.16).

Only he who lives by the forgiveness of his sin in Jesus Christ will rightly think little of himself. He will know that his own wisdom reached the end of its tether when Jesus forgave him. He remembers the ambition of the first man who wanted to know what is good and evil and perished in his wisdom. That first man who was born on this earth was Cain, the fratricide. His crime is the fruit of man's wisdom. Because the Christian can no longer fancy that he is wise he will also have no high opinion of his own schemes and plans. He will know that it is good for his own will to be broken in the encounter with his neighbour. He will be ready to consider his neighbour's will more important and urgent than his own. What does it matter if our own plans are frustrated? Is it not better to serve our neighbour than to have our own way?

But not only my neighbour's will, but also his honour is more important than mine. 'How can ye believe, which receive honour one of another, and seek not the honour that cometh from God only?' (John 5.44). The desire for one's own honour hinders faith. One who seeks his own honour is no longer seeking God and his neighbour. What does it matter if I suffer injustice? Would I not have deserved even worse punishment from God, if he had not dealt with me according to his mercy? Is not justice done to me a thousand times even in injustice? Must it not be wholesome and conducive to humility for me to learn to bear such petty evils silently and patiently? 'The patient in spirit is better than the proud in spirit' (Eccl. 7.8).

One who lives by justification by grace is willing and ready to accept even insults and injuries without protest, taking them from God's punishing and gracious hand. It is not a good sign when we can no longer bear to hear this said without immediately retorting that even Paul insisted upon his rights as a Roman citizen, and that Jesus replied to the man who struck him, 'Why smitest thou me?' In any case, none of us will really act as Jesus and Paul did if we have not first learned, like them, to keep silent under abuse. The sin of resentment that flares up so quickly in the fellowship indicates again and again how much false desire for honour, how much unbelief, still smoulders in the community.

Finally, one extreme thing must be said. To forgo self-conceit and to associate with the lowly means, in all soberness and without mincing the matter, to consider oneself the greatest of sinners. This arouses all the resistance of the natural man, but also that of the self-confident Christian. It sounds like an exaggeration, like an untruth. Yet even Paul said of himself that he was the foremost of sinners (I Tim. 1.15); he said this specifically at the point where he was speaking of his service as an apostle. There can be no genuine acknowledgment of sin that does not lead to this extremity. If my sinfulness appears to me to be in any way smaller or less detestable in comparison with the sins of others, I am still not recognizing my sinfulness at all. My sin is of necessity the worst, the most grievous, the most reprehensible. Brotherly love will find any number of extenuations for the sins of others; only for my sin is there no apology whatsoever. Therefore my sin is the worst. He who would serve his brother in the fellowship must sink all the way down to these depths of humility. How can I possibly serve another person in unfeigned humility if I seriously regard his sinfulness as worse than my own? Would I not be putting myself above him; could I have any hope for him? Such service would be hypocritical. 'Never think that thou hast made any progress till thou look upon thyself as inferior to all' (Thomas à Kempis).

How, then, is true brotherly service performed in the Christian community? We are apt these days to reply too quickly that the one real service to our neighbour is to

minister to him the Word of God. It is true that there is no
service that compares with this one, and even more, that
every other service is performed for the sake of the service
of the Word of God. Yet a Christian community does not
consist solely of preachers of the Word. We can go mon-
strously wrong here if we overlook a number of other
things.

The Ministry of Listening

The first service that one owes to others in the fellowship consists in listening to them. Just as love to God begins
with listening to his Word, so the beginning of love for the
brethren is learning to listen to them. It is God's love for
us that he not only gives us his Word but also lends us his
ear. So it is his work that we do for our brother when we
learn to listen to him. Christians, especially ministers, so
often think they must always contribute something when
they are in the company of others, that this is the one service they have to render. They forget that listening can be
a greater service than speaking.

Many people are looking for an ear that will listen. They
do not find it among Christians, because these Christians
are talking where they should be listening. But he who can
no longer listen to his brother will soon be no longer listening to God either; he will be doing nothing but prattle in
the presence of God too. This is the beginning of the death
of the spiritual life, and in the end there is nothing left but
spiritual chatter and clerical condescension arrayed in
pious words. One who cannot listen long and patiently will
presently be talking beside the point and be never really
speaking to others, albeit he be not conscious of it. Anyone
who thinks that his time is too valuable to spend keeping
quiet will eventually have no time for God and his brother,
but only for himself and for his own follies.

Brotherly pastoral care is essentially distinguished from
preaching by the fact that, added to the task of speaking the
Word, there is the obligation of listening. There is a kind

of listening with half an ear that presumes already to know what the other person has to say. It is an impatient, inattentive listening, that despises the brother and is only waiting for a chance to speak and so get rid of the other person. This is no fulfilment of our obligation, and it is certain that here too our attitude toward our brother only reflects our relationship to God. It is little wonder that we are no longer capable of the greatest service of listening that God has committed to us, that of hearing our brother's confession, if we refuse to give ear to our brother on lesser subjects. Secular education today is aware that often a person can be helped merely by having someone who will listen to him seriously, and upon this insight it has constructed its own soul therapy, which has attracted great numbers of people, including Christians. But Christians have forgotten that the ministry of listening has been committed to them by him who is himself the great listener and whose work they should share. We should listen with the ears of God that we may speak the Word of God.

The Ministry of Helpfulness

The second service that one should perform for another in a Christian community is that of active helpfulness. This means, initially, simple assistance in trifling, external matters. There is a multitude of these things wherever people live together. Nobody is too good for the meanest service. One who worries about the loss of time that such petty, outward acts of helpfulness entail is usually taking the importance of his own career too solemnly.

We must be ready to allow ourselves to be interrupted by God. God will be constantly crossing our paths and cancelling our plans by sending us people with claims and petitions. We may pass them by, preoccupied with our more important tasks, as the priest passed by the man who had fallen among thieves, perhaps—reading the Bible. When we do that we pass by the visible sign of the Cross raised athwart our path to show us that, not our way, but God's way must be done. It is a strange fact that Christians and even ministers frequently consider their work so important and urgent that they will allow nothing to disturb them. They think they are doing God a service in this, but actually they are disdaining God's 'crooked yet straight path' (Gottfried Arnold). They do not want a life that is crossed and balked. But it is part of the discipline of humility that we must not spare our hand where it can perform a service and that we do not assume that our schedule is our own to manage, but allow it to be arranged by God.

In the monastery his vow of obedience to the abbot deprives the monk of the right to dispose of his own time. In evangelical community life, free service to one's brother takes the place of the vow. Only where hands are not too good for deeds of love and mercy in everyday helpfulness can the mouth joyfully and convincingly proclaim the message of God's love and mercy.

The Ministry of Bearing

We speak, third, of the service that consists in bearing others. 'Bear ye one another's burdens, and so fulfil the law of Christ' (Gal. 6.2). Thus the law of Christ is a law of bearing. Bearing means forbearing and sustaining. The brother is a burden to the Christian, precisely because he is a Christian. For the pagan the other person never becomes a burden at all. He simply sidesteps every burden that others may impose upon him.

The Christian, however, must bear the burden of a brother. He must suffer and endure the brother. It is only when he is a burden that another person is really a brother and not merely an object to be manipulated. The burden of men was so heavy for God himself that he had to endure the Cross. God verily bore the burden of men in the body of Jesus Christ. But he bore them as a mother carries her child, as a shepherd enfolds a lost lamb that has been found. God took men upon himself and they weighted him to the ground, but God remained with them and they with God. In bearing with men God maintained fellowship with them. It is the law of Christ that was fulfilled in the Cross. And Christians must share in this law. They must suffer their brethren, but, what is more important, now that the law of Christ has been fulfilled, they *can* bear with their brethren.

The Bible speaks with remarkable frequency of 'bearing'. It is capable of expressing the whole work of Jesus Christ in this one word. 'Surely he hath borne our griefs, and carried our sorrows . . . the chastisement of our peace was upon him' (Isa. 53.4-5). Therefore, the Bible can also characterize the whole life of the Christian as bearing the Cross. It is the fellowship of the Cross to experience the burden of the other. If one does not experience it, the fellowship he belongs to is not Christian. If any member refuses to bear that burden, he denies the law of Christ.

It is, first of all, the *freedom* of the other person, of which we spoke earlier, that is a burden to the Christian. The other's freedom collides with his own autonomy, yet he must recognize it. He could get rid of this burden by refusing the other person his freedom, by constraining him and thus doing violence to his personality, by stamping his own image upon him. But if he lets God create his image in him, he by this token gives him his freedom and himself bears the burden of this freedom of another creature of God. The freedom of the other person includes all that we mean by a person's nature, individuality, endowment. It also includes his weaknesses and oddities, which are such a trial to our patience, everything that produces frictions, conflicts, and collisions among us. To bear the burden of the other person means involvement with the created reality of the other, to accept and affirm it, and, in bearing with it, to break through to the point where we take joy in it.

This will prove especially difficult where varying

strength and weakness in faith are bound together in a fellowship. The weak must not judge the strong, the strong must not despise the weak. The weak must guard against pride, the strong against indifference. None must seek his own rights. If the strong person falls, the weak one must guard his heart against malicious joy at his downfall. If the weak one falls, the strong one must help him rise again in all kindness. The one needs as much patience as the other. 'Woe to him that is alone when he falleth; for he hath not another to help him up' (Eccl. 4.10). It is doubtless this bearing of another person in his freedom that the Scripture means when it speaks of 'forbearing one another' (Col. 3.13). 'Walk with all lowliness and meekness, with longsuffering, forbearing one another in love' (Eph. 4.2).

Then, besides the other's freedom, there is the abuse of that freedom that becomes a burden for the Christian. The sin of the other person is harder to bear than his freedom; for in sin, fellowship with God and with the brother is broken. Here the Christian suffers the rupture of his fellowship with the other person that had its basis in Jesus Christ. But here, too, it is only in bearing with him that the great grace of God becomes wholly plain. To cherish no contempt for the sinner but rather to prize the privilege of bearing him means not to have to give him up as lost, to be able to accept him, to preserve the fellowship with him through forgiveness. 'Brethren, if a man be overtaken in a fault, ye which are spiritual, restore such an one in the spirit of meekness' (Gal. 6.1). As Christ bore and received us as sinners so we in his fellowship may bear and receive sinners into the fellowship of Jesus Christ through the forgiving of sins.

We may suffer the sins of our brother; we do not need to judge. This is a mercy for the Christian; for when does sin ever occur in the community that he must not examine and blame himself for his own unfaithfulness in prayer and intercession, his lack of brotherly service, of fraternal reproof and encouragement, indeed, for his own personal sin and spiritual laxity, by which he has done injury to himself, the fellowship, and the brethren? Since every sin of every member burdens and indicts the whole community, the congregation rejoices, in the midst of all the pain and the burden the brother's sin inflicts, that it has the privilege of bearing and forgiving. 'Behold, you bear them all, and likewise all of them bear you, and all things are common, both the good and the bad' (Luther).

The service of forgiveness is rendered by one to the others daily. It occurs, without words, in the intercessions for one another. And every member of the fellowship, who does not grow weary in this ministry, can depend upon it that this service is also being rendered him by the brethren. He who is bearing others knows that he himself is being borne, and only in this strength can he go on bearing.

Then where the ministry of listening, active helpfulness, and bearing with others is faithfully performed, the ultimate and highest service can also be rendered, namely, the ministry of the Word of God.

The Ministry of Proclaiming

What we are concerned with here is the free communication of the Word from person to person, not by the ordained ministry which is bound to a particular office, time, and place. We are thinking of that unique situation in which one person bears witness in human words to another person, bespeaking the whole consolation of God, the admonition, the kindness, and the severity of God. The speaking of that Word is beset with infinite perils. If it is not accompanied by worthy listening, how can it really be the right word for the other person? If it is contradicted by one's own lack of active helpfulness, how can it be a convincing and sincere word? If it issues, not from a spirit of bearing and forbearing, but from impatience and the desire to force its acceptance, how can it be the liberating and healing word?

Moreover, the person who has really listened and served and borne with others is the very one who is likely to say nothing. A profound distrust of everything that is merely verbal often causes a personal word to a brother to be suppressed. What can weak human words accomplish for others? Why add to the empty talk? Are we, like the professionally pious, to 'talk away' the other person's real need? Is there anything more perilous than speaking God's Word to excess? But, on the other hand, who wants to be accountable for having been silent when he should have spoken? How much easier is ordered speech in the pulpit than this entirely free speech which is uttered betwixt the responsibility to be silent and the responsibility to speak!

Added to the fear of one's responsibility to speak there is the fear of the other person. What a difficult thing it often is to utter the name of Jesus Christ in the presence even of a brother! Here, too, it is difficult to distinguish between right and wrong. Who dares to force himself upon his neighbour? Who is entitled to accost and confront his neighbour and talk to him about ultimate matters? It would be no sign of great Christian insight were one simply to say at this point that everybody has this right, indeed, this obligation. This could be the point where the desire to dominate might again assert itself in the most insidious way. The other person, as a matter of fact, has his own right, his own responsibility, and even his own duty, to defend himself against unauthorized interference. The other person has his own secret which dare not be invaded without great injury, and which he cannot surrender without destroying himself. It is not a secret dependent on knowledge or feeling, but rather the secret of his freedom, his salvation, his being. And yet this correct judgment lies perilously near to the deadly dictum of Cain: 'Am I my brother's keeper?' A seemingly sacred respect for another's freedom can be subject to the curse of God: 'His blood will I require at thine hand' (Ezek. 3.18).

Where Christians live together the time must inevitably

come when in some crisis one person will have to declare God's Word and will to another. It is inconceivable that the things that are of utmost importance to each individual should not be spoken by one to another. It is unchristian consciously to deprive another of the one decisive service we can render to him. If we cannot bring ourselves to utter it, we shall have to ask ourselves whether we are not still seeing our brother garbed in his human dignity which we are afraid to touch, and thus forgetting the most important thing, that he, too, no matter how old or highly placed or distinguished he may be, is still a man like us, a sinner in crying need of God's grace. He has the same great necessities that we have, and needs help, encouragement, and forgiveness as we do.

the
basis

The basis upon which Christians can speak to one another is that each knows the other as a sinner, who, with all his human dignity, is lonely and lost if he is not given help. This is not to make him contemptible nor to disparage him in any way. On the contrary, it is to accord him the one real dignity that man has, namely, that, though he is a sinner, he can share in God's grace and glory and be God's child. This recognition gives to our brotherly speech the freedom and candour that it needs. We speak to one another on the basis of the help we both need. We admonish one another to go the way that Christ bids us to go. We warn one another against the disobedience that is our common destruction. We are gentle and we are severe with one another, for we know both God's kindness and God's severity. Why should we be afraid of one another, since both of us have only God to fear? Why should we think that our brother would not understand us, when we understood very well what was meant when somebody spoke God's comfort or God's admonition to us, perhaps in words that were halting and unskilled? Or do we really think there is a single person in this world who does not need either encouragement or admonition? Why, then, has God bestowed Christian brotherhood upon us?

The more we learn to allow others to speak the Word to us, to accept humbly and gratefully even severe reproaches and admonitions, the more free and objective will we be in speaking ourselves. The person whose touchiness and vanity make him spurn a brother's earnest censure cannot speak the truth in humility to others; he is afraid of being rebuffed and of feeling that he has been aggrieved. The touchy person will always become a flatterer and very soon he will come to despise and slander his brother. But the humble person will stick to both truth and love. He will stick to the Word of God and let it lead him to his brother. Because he seeks nothing for himself and has no fears for himself, he can help his brother through the Word.

Reproof is unavoidable. God's Word demands it when a brother falls into open sin. The practice of discipline in the congregation begins in the smallest circles. Where defection from God's Word in doctrine or life imperils the family fellowship and with it the whole congregation, the word of admonition and rebuke must be ventured. Nothing can be more cruel than the tenderness that consigns another to his sin. Nothing can be more compassionate than the severe rebuke that calls a brother back from the path of sin. It is a ministry of mercy, an ultimate offer of genuine fellowship, when we allow nothing but God's Word to stand between us, judging and succouring. Then it is not we who are judging; God alone judges, and God's judgment is helpful and healing. Ultimately, we have no charge but to serve our brother, never to set ourselves above him, and we serve him even when we must speak the judging and dividing Word of God to him, even when, in obedience to God, we must break off fellowship with him. We must know that it is not our human love which makes us loyal to the other person, but God's love which breaks its way through to him only through judgment. Just because God's Word judges, it serves the person. He who accepts the ministry of God's judgment is helped. This is the point where the limitations of all human action toward our brother become apparent: 'None of them can by any means redeem his brother, nor give to God a ransom for him (for the redemption of their life is costly, and it faileth for ever)' (Ps. 49.7-8 A.R.V.).

This renunciation of our own ability is precisely the prerequisite and the sanction for the redeeming help that only the Word of God can give to the brother. Our brother's ways are not in our hands; we cannot hold together what is breaking; we cannot keep life in what is determined to die. But God binds elements together in the breaking, creates community in the separation, grants grace through judgment. He has put his Word in our mouth. He wants it to be spoken through us. If we hinder his Word, the blood of the sinning brother will be upon us. If we carry out his Word, God will save our brother through us. 'He which converteth the sinner from the error of his ways shall save a soul from death, and shall hide a multitude of sins' (James 5.20).

The Ministry of Authority

'Whosoever will be great among you, shall be your minister' (Mark 10.43). Jesus made authority in the fellowship dependent upon brotherly service. Genuine spiritual authority is to be found only where the ministry of hearing, helping, bearing, and proclaiming is carried out. Every cult of personality that emphasizes the distinguished qualities, virtues, and talents of another person, even though these be of an altogether spiritual nature, is worldly and has no place in the Christian community; indeed, it poisons the Christian community. The desire we so often hear expressed today for 'episcopal figures', 'priestly men', 'authoritative personalities' springs frequently enough from a spiritually sick need for the admiration of men, for the establishment of visible human authority, because the genuine authority of service appears to be so unimpressive. There is nothing that so sharply contradicts such a desire as the New Testa-

ment itself in its description of a bishop (I Tim. 3.1ff.).
One finds there nothing whatsoever with respect to worldly
charm and the brilliant attributes of a spiritual personality.
The bishop is a simple, faithful man, sound in faith and
life, who rightly discharges his duties to the Church. His
authority lies in the exercise of his ministry. In the man
himself there is nothing to admire.

Ultimately, this hankering for false authority has at its
root a desire to re-establish some sort of immediacy, a
dependence upon human beings in the Church. Genuine
authority knows that all immediacy is especially baneful
in matters of authority. Genuine authority realizes that it
can exist only in the service of him who alone has authority. Genuine authority knows that it is bound in the
strictest sense by the saying of Jesus: 'One is your Master,
even Christ; and all ye are brethren' (Matt. 23.8). The
Church does not need brilliant personalities but faithful
servants of Jesus and the brethren. Not in the former but
in the latter is the lack. The Church will place its confidence only in the simple servant of the Word of Jesus
Christ because it knows that then it will be guided, not
according to human wisdom and human conceit, but by
the Word of the Good Shepherd.

The question of trust, which is so closely related to that
of authority, is determined by the faithfulness with which
a man serves Jesus Christ, never by the extraordinary
talents which he possesses. Pastoral authority can be at-
tained only by the servant of Jesus who seeks no power of
his own, who himself is a brother among brothers sub-
mitted to the authority of the Word.

V

Confession and Communion

'CONFESS YOUR faults one to another' (James 5.16). He who is alone with his sin is utterly alone. It may be that Christians, notwithstanding corporate worship, common prayer, and all their fellowship in service, may still be left to their loneliness. The final break-through to fellowship does not occur, because, though they have fellowship with one another as believers and as devout people, they do not have fellowship as the undevout, as sinners. The pious fellowship permits no one to be a sinner. So everybody must conceal his sin from himself and from the fellowship. We dare not be sinners. Many Christians are unthinkably horrified when a real sinner is suddenly discovered among the righteous. So we remain alone with our sin, living in lies and hypocrisy. The fact is that we *are* sinners!

But it is the grace of the Gospel, which is so hard for the pious to understand, that it confronts us with the truth and says: You are a sinner, a great, desperate sinner; now come, as the sinner that you are, to God who loves you. He wants you as you are; he does not want anything from you, a sacrifice, a work; he wants you alone. 'My son, give me thine heart' (Prov. 23.26). God has come to you to save the sinner. Be glad! This message is liberation through truth. You can hide nothing from God. The mask you wear before men will do you no good before him. He wants to see you as you are, he wants to be gracious to you. You do not have to go on lying to yourself and your brothers, as if you were without sin; you can dare to be a sinner. Thank God for that; he loves the sinner but he hates sin.

Christ became our Brother in the flesh in order that we might believe in him. In him the love of God came to the sinner. Through him men could be sinners and only so could they be helped. All sham was ended in the presence of Christ. The misery of the sinner and the mercy of God— this was the truth of the Gospel in Jesus Christ. It was in this truth that his Church was to live. Therefore, he gave his followers the authority to hear the confession of sin and to forgive sin in his name. 'Whose soever sins ye remit, they are remitted unto them; and whose soever sins ye retain, they are retained' (John 20.23).

When he did that Christ made the Church, and in it our brother, a blessing to us. Now our brother stands in Christ's stead. Before him I need no longer to dissemble. Before him alone in the whole world I dare to be the sinner that I am; here the truth of Jesus Christ and his mercy rules. Christ became our Brother in order to help us. Through him our brother has become Christ for us in the power and authority of the commission Christ has given to him. Our brother stands before us as the sign of the truth and the grace of God. He has been given to us to help us. He hears the confession of our sins in Christ's stead and he forgives our sins in Christ's name. He keeps the secret of our confession as God keeps it. When I go to my brother to confess, I am going to God.

So in the Christian community when the call to brotherly confession and forgiveness goes forth it is a call to the great grace of God in the Church.

Breaking Through to Community

In confession the break-through to community takes place. Sin demands to have a man by himself. It withdraws him from the community. The more isolated a person is, the more destructive will be the power of sin over him, and the more deeply he becomes involved in it, the more disastrous is his isolation. Sin wants to remain unknown. It shuns the light. In the darkness of the unexpressed it poisons the whole being of a person. This can happen even in the midst of a pious community. In confession the light of the Gospel breaks into the darkness and seclusion of the heart. The sin must be brought into the light. The unexpressed must be openly spoken and acknowledged. All that is secret and hidden is made manifest. It is a hard struggle until the sin is openly admitted. But God breaks gates of brass and bars of iron (Ps. 107.16).

Since the confession of sin is made in the presence of a Christian brother, the last stronghold of self-justification is abandoned. The sinner surrenders; he gives up all his evil. He gives his heart to God, and he finds the forgiveness of all his sin in the fellowship of Jesus Christ and his brother. The expressed, acknowledged sin has lost all its power. It has been revealed and judged as sin. It can no longer tear the fellowship asunder. Now the fellowship bears the sin of the brother. He is no longer alone with his evil for he has cast off his sin in confession and handed it over to God. It has been taken away from him. Now he stands in the fellowship of sinners who live by the grace of God in the Cross of Jesus Christ. Now he can be a sinner and still enjoy the grace of God. He can confess his sins and in this very act find fellowship for the first time. The sin concealed separated him from the fellowship, made all his apparent fellowship a sham; the sin confessed has helped him to find true fellowship with the brethren in Jesus Christ.

Moreover, what we have said applies solely to confession between two Christians. A confession of sin in the presence of all the members of the congregation is not required to restore one to fellowship with the whole congregation. I meet the whole congregation in the one brother to whom I confess my sins and who forgives my sins. In the fellowship I find with this one brother I have already found fellowship with the whole congregation. In this matter no one acts in his own name nor by his own authority, but by the commission of Jesus Christ. This commission is given to

the whole congregation and the individual is called merely
to exercise it for the congregation. If a Christian is in the
fellowship of confession with a brother he will never be
alone again, anywhere.

Breaking Through to the Cross

In confession occurs the break-through to the Cross. The
root of all sin is pride, *superbia*. I want to be my own law,
I have a right to my self, my hatred and my desires, my
life and my death. The mind and flesh of man are set on fire
by pride; for it is precisely in his wickedness that man
wants to be as God. Confession in the presence of a brother
is the profoundest kind of humiliation. It hurts, it cuts a
man down, it is a dreadful blow to pride. To stand there
before a brother as a sinner is an ignominy that is almost
unbearable. In the confession of concrete sins the old man
dies a painful, shameful death before the eyes of a brother.
Because this humiliation is so hard we continually scheme
to evade confessing to a brother. Our eyes are so blinded
that they no longer see the promise and the glory in such
abasement.

It was none other than Jesus Christ himself who suffered
the scandalous, public death of a sinner in our stead. He
was not ashamed to be crucified for us as an evildoer. It
is nothing else but our fellowship with Jesus Christ that
leads us to the ignominious dying that comes in confession,
in order that we may in truth share in his Cross. The Cross
of Jesus Christ destroys all pride. We cannot find the
Cross of Jesus if we shrink from going to the place where
it is to be found, namely, the public death of the sinner.
And we refuse to bear the Cross when we are ashamed to
take upon ourselves the shameful death of the sinner in
confession. In confession we break through to the true
fellowship of the Cross of Jesus Christ, in confession we
affirm and accept our cross. In the deep mental and physical pain of humiliation before a brother—which means,
before God—we experience the Cross of Jesus as our res-

cue and salvation. The old man dies, but it is God who has conquered him. Now we share in the resurrection of Christ and eternal life.

Breaking Through to New Life

In confession the break-through to new life occurs. Where sin is hated, admitted, and forgiven, there the break with the past is made. 'Old things are passed away.' But where there is a break with sin, there is conversion. Confession is conversion. 'Behold, all things are become new' (II Cor. 5.17). Christ has made a new beginning with us.

As the first disciples left all and followed when Jesus called, so in confession the Christian gives up all and follows. Confession is discipleship. Life with Jesus Christ and his community has begun. 'He that covereth his sins shall not prosper: but whoso confesseth and forsaketh them shall have mercy' (Prov. 28.13). In confession the Christian begins to forsake his sins. Their domination is broken. From now on the Christian wins victory after victory.

What happened to us in baptism is bestowed upon us anew in confession. We are delivered out of darkness into the kingdom of Jesus Christ. That is joyful news. Confession is the renewal of the joy of baptism. 'Weeping may endure for a night, but joy cometh in the morning' (Ps. 30.5).

Breaking Through to Certainty

In confession a man breaks through to certainty. Why is it that it is often easier for us to confess our sins to God than to a brother? God is holy and sinless, he is a just judge of evil and the enemy of all disobedience. But a brother is sinful as we are. He knows from his own experience the dark night of secret sin. Why should we not find it easier to go to a brother than to the holy God? But if we do, we must ask ourselves whether we have not often been deceiving ourselves with our confession of sin to God, whether we have not rather been confessing our sins to ourselves and also granting ourselves absolution. And is not the reason perhaps for our countless relapses and the feebleness of our Christian obedience to be found precisely in the fact that we are living on self-forgiveness and not a real forgiveness? Self-forgiveness can never lead to a breach with sin; this can be accomplished only by the judging and pardoning Word of God itself.

Who can give us the certainty that, in the confession and the forgiveness of our sins, we are not dealing with ourselves but with the living God? God gives us this certainty through our brother. Our brother breaks the circle of self-deception. A man who confesses his sins in the presence of a brother knows that he is no longer alone with himself; he experiences the presence of God in the reality of the other person. As long as I am by myself in the confession of my sins everything remains in the dark, but in the presence of a brother the sin has to be brought into the light. But since the sin must come to light some time, it is better that it happens today between me and my brother, rather than on the last day in the piercing light of the final judgment. It is a mercy that we can confess our sins to a brother. Such grace spares us the terrors of the last judgment.

Our brother has been given me that even here and now I may be made certain through him of the reality of God in his judgment and his grace. As the open confession of my sins to a brother insures me against self-deception, so, too, the assurance of forgiveness becomes fully certain to me only when it is spoken by a brother in the name of God. Mutual, brotherly confession is given to us by God in order that we may be sure of divine forgiveness.

But it is precisely for the sake of this certainty that confession should deal with *concrete* sins. People usually are satisfied when they make a general confession. But one experiences the utter perdition and corruption of human nature, in so far as this ever enters into experience at all, when one sees his own specific sins. Self-examination on the basis of all Ten Commandments will therefore be the right preparation for confession. Otherwise it might happen that one could still be a hypocrite even in confessing to a brother and thus miss the good of the confession. Jesus dealt with people whose sins were obvious, with publicans and harlots. They knew why they needed forgiveness, and they received it as forgiveness of their specific sins. Blind Bartimaeus was asked by Jesus: What do you want me to do for you? Before confession we must have a clear answer to this question. In confession we, too, receive the forgiveness of the particular sins which are here brought to light, and by this very token the forgiveness of our sins, known and unknown.

Does all this mean that confession to a brother is a divine law? No, confession is not a law, it is an offer of divine help for the sinner. It is possible that a person may by God's grace break through to certainty, new life, the Cross, and fellowship without benefit of confession to a brother. It is possible that a person may never know what it is to doubt his own forgiveness and despair of his own confession of sin, that he may be given everything in his own private confession to God. We have spoken here for those who cannot make this assertion. Luther himself was one of those for whom the Christian life was unthinkable without mutual, brotherly confession. In the *Large Catechism* he said: 'Therefore when I admonish you to confession I am admonishing you to be a Christian'. Those who, despite all their seeking and trying, cannot find the great joy of fellowship, the Cross, the new life, and certainty should be shown the blessing that God offers us in mutual confession. Confession is within the liberty of the Christian. Who can refuse, without suffering loss, a help that God has deemed it necessary to offer?

To Whom Confess?

To whom shall we make confession? According to Jesus' promise, every Christian brother can hear the confession of another. But will he understand? May he not be so far above us in his Christian life that he would only turn away from us with no understanding of our personal sins?

Anybody who lives beneath the Cross and who has discerned in the Cross of Jesus the utter wickedness of all men and of his own heart will find there is no sin that can ever be alien to him. Anybody who has once been horrified by the dreadfulness of his own sin that nailed Jesus to the Cross will no longer be horrified by even the rankest sins of a brother. Looking at the Cross of Jesus, he knows the human heart. He knows how utterly lost it is in sin and weakness, how it goes astray in the ways of sin, and he also knows that it is accepted in grace and mercy. Only the brother under the Cross can hear a confession.

It is not experience of life but experience of the Cross that makes one a worthy hearer of confessions. The most experienced psychologist or observer of human nature knows infinitely less of the human heart than the simplest Christian who lives beneath the Cross of Jesus. The greatest psychological insight, ability, and experience cannot grasp this one thing: what sin is. Worldly wisdom knows what distress and weakness and failure are, but it does not know the godlessness of men. And so it also does not know that man is destroyed only by his sin and can be healed only by forgiveness. Only the Christian knows this. In the presence of a psychiatrist I can only be a sick man; in the presence of a Christian brother I can dare to be a sinner. The psychiatrist must first search my heart and yet he never plumbs its ultimate depth. The Christian brother knows when I come to him: here is a sinner like myself, a godless man who wants to confess and yearns for God's forgiveness. The psychiatrist views me as if there were no God. The brother views me as I am before the judging and merciful God in the Cross of Jesus Christ. It is not lack of psychological knowledge but lack of love for the crucified Jesus Christ that makes us so poor and inefficient in brotherly confession.

In daily, earnest living with the Cross of Christ the Christian loses the spirit of human censoriousness on the one hand and weak indulgence on the other, and he receives the spirit of divine severity and divine love. The death of the sinner before God and life that comes out of that death through grace become for him a daily reality. So he loves the brothers with the merciful love of God that leads through the death of the sinner to the life of the child of God. Who can hear our confession? He who himself lives beneath the Cross. Wherever the message concerning the Crucified is a vital, living thing, there brotherly confession will also avail.

Two Dangers

There are two dangers that a Christian community which practises confession must guard against. The first concerns the one who hears confessions. It is not a good thing for one person to be the confessor for all the others. All too easily this one person will be overburdened; thus confession will become for him an empty routine, and this will give rise to the disastrous misuse of the confessional for the exercise of spiritual domination of souls. In order that he may not succumb to this sinister danger of the confessional every person should refrain from listening to confession who does not himself practise it. Only the person who has so humbled himself can hear a brother's confession without harm.

The second danger concerns the confessant. For the salvation of his soul let him guard against ever making a pious work of his confession. If he does so, it will become the final, most abominable, vicious, and impure prostitution of the heart; the act becomes an idle, lustful babbling. Confession as a pious work is an invention of the devil. It is only God's offer of grace, help and forgiveness that could make us dare to enter the abyss of confession. We can confess solely for the sake of the promise of absolution. Confession as a routine duty is spiritual death; confession in reliance upon the promise is life. The forgiveness of sins is the sole ground and goal of confession.

The Joyful Sacrament

Though it is true that confession is an act in the name of Christ that is complete in itself and is exercised in the fellowship as frequently as there is desire for it, it serves the Christian community especially as a preparation for the common reception of the holy Communion. Reconciled to God and men, Christians desire to receive the body and blood of Jesus Christ. It is the command of Jesus that none should come to the altar with a heart that is unreconciled to his brother. If this command of Jesus applies to every service of worship, indeed, to every prayer we utter, then it most certainly applies to reception of the Lord's Supper.

The day before the Lord's Supper is administered will find the brethren of a Christian fellowship together and each will beg the forgiveness of the others for the wrongs committed. Nobody who avoids this approach to his brother can go rightly prepared to the table of the Lord. All anger, strife, envy, evil gossip, and unbrotherly conduct must have been settled and finished if the brethren wish to receive the grace of God together in the sacrament. But to beg a brother's pardon is still not confession, and only the latter is subject to the express command of Jesus.

But preparation for the Lord's Supper will also awaken in the individual the desire to be completely certain that the particular sins which disturb and torment him and are known only to God are forgiven. It is this desire that the offer of brotherly confession and absolution fulfils. Where there is deep anxiety and trouble over one's own sins, where the certainty of forgiveness is sought, there comes the invitation in the name of Jesus to come to brotherly confession. What brought upon Jesus the accusation of blasphemy, namely, that he forgave sinners, is what now takes place in the Christian brotherhood in the power of the presence of Jesus Christ. One forgives the other all his sins in the name of the triune God. And there is joy in the presence of the angels of God over the sinner who repents. Hence the time of preparation for the Lord's Supper will be filled with brotherly admonition and encouragement, with prayers, with fear, and with joy.

The day of the Lord's Supper is an occasion of joy for the Christian community. Reconciled in their hearts with God and the brethren, the congregation receives the gift of the body and blood of Jesus Christ, and, receiving that, it receives forgiveness, new life, and salvation. It is given new fellowship with God and men. The fellowship of the Lord's Supper is the superlative fulfilment of Christian fellowship. As the members of the congregation are united in body and blood at the table of the Lord so will they be together in eternity. Here the community has reached its goal. Here joy in Christ and his community is complete. The life of Christians together under the Word has reached its perfection in the sacrament.